MACMILLAN MASTER GUIDES

General Editor: James Gibson

Published:

JANE AUSTEN: **PRIDE AND PREJUDICE** Ra
          EMMA Norman Page
          MANSFIELD PARK Richard
ROBERT BOLT: **A MAN FOR ALL SEASONS**
EMILY BRONTË: **WUTHERING HEIGHTS** Hil
GEOFFREY CHAUCER: **THE PROLOGUE TO THE CANTERBURY TALES**
          Nigel Thomas and Richard Swan
          THE MILLER'S TALE Michael Alexander
CHARLES DICKENS: **BLEAK HOUSE** Dennis Butts
          GREAT EXPECTATIONS Dennis Butts
          HARD TIMES Norman Page
GEORGE ELIOT: **MIDDLEMARCH** Graham Handley
          SILAS MARNER Graham Handley
E. M. FORSTER: **A PASSAGE TO INDIA** Hilda D. Spear
THE METAPHYSICAL POETS Joan van Emden
WILLIAM GOLDING: **LORD OF THE FLIES** Raymond Wilson
OLIVER GOLDSMITH: **SHE STOOPS TO CONQUER** Paul Ranger
THOMAS HARDY: **FAR FROM THE MADDING CROWD** Colin Temblett-Wood
          TESS OF THE D'URBERVILLES James Gibson
CHRISTOPHER MARLOWE: **DOCTOR FAUSTUS** David A. Male
ARTHUR MILLER: **THE CRUCIBLE** Leonard Smith
GEORGE ORWELL: **ANIMAL FARM** Jean Armstrong
WILLIAM SHAKESPEARE: **MACBETH** David Elloway
          A MIDSUMMER NIGHT'S DREAM Kenneth Pickering
          ROMEO AND JULIET Helen Morris
          THE WINTER'S TALE Diana Devlin
          HENRY IV PART I Helen Morris
GEORGE BERNARD SHAW: **ST JOAN** Leonée Ormond
RICHARD SHERIDAN: **THE RIVALS** Jeremy Rowe
          THE SCHOOL FOR SCANDAL Paul Ranger

Forthcoming:

SAMUEL BECKETT: **WAITING FOR GODOT** J. Birkett
WILLIAM BLAKE: **SONGS OF INNOCENCE AND SONGS OF EXPERIENCE**
          A. Tomlinson
GEORGE ELIOT: **THE MILL ON THE FLOSS** H. Wheeler
T. S. ELIOT: **MURDER IN THE CATHEDRAL** P. Lapworth
HENRY FIELDING: **JOSEPH ANDREWS** T. Johnson
E. M. FORSTER: **HOWARD'S END** I. Milligan
WILLIAM GOLDING: **THE SPIRE** R. Sumner
THOMAS HARDY: **THE MAYOR OF CASTERBRIDGE** R. Evans
SELECTED POEMS OF GERALD MANLEY HOPKINS
PHILIP LARKIN: **THE WHITSUN WEDDING AND THE LESS DECEIVED**
          A. Swarbrick
D. H. LAWRENCE: **SONS AND LOVERS** R. Draper
HARPER LEE: **TO KILL A MOCKINGBIRD** Jean Armstrong
THOMAS MIDDLETON: **THE CHANGELING** A. Bromham
ARTHUR MILLER: **DEATH OF A SALESMAN** P. Spalding
WILLIAM SHAKESPEARE: **HAMLET** J. Brooks
          HENRY V P. Davison
          KING LEAR F. Casey
          JULIUS CAESAR David Elloway
          MEASURE FOR MEASURE M. Lilly
          OTHELLO Christopher Beddows
          RICHARD II C. Barber
          TWELFTH NIGHT Edward Leeson
          THE TEMPEST Kenneth Pickering
TWO PLAYS OF JOHN WEBSTER David A. Male

Also published by Macmillan

MASTERING ENGLISH LITERATURE R. Gill
MASTERING ENGLISH LANGUAGE S. H. Burton
MASTERING ENGLISH GRAMMAR S. H. Burton

WORK OUT SERIES
WORK OUT ENGLISH LANGUAGE ('O' level and GCSE) S. H. Burton
WORK OUT ENGLISH LITERATURE ('A' level) S. H. Burton

MACMILLAN MASTER GUIDES

ST JOAN

BY GEORGE BERNARD SHAW

LEONÉE ORMOND

MACMILLAN

First edition 1986

Published by
MACMILLAN EDUCATION LTD
Houndmills, Basingstoke, Hampshire RG21 2XS
and London
Companies and representatives
throughout the world

Typeset by
TECSET, Sutton, Surrey

Printed in Hong Kong

British Library Cataloguing in Publication Data
Ormond, Leonée
St Joan by George Bernard Shaw. — (Macmillan
master guides)
1. Shaw, Bernard, Saint Joan
I. Title   II. Shaw, Bernard
822′912   PR5363.S33
ISBN 0-333-37940-3 Pbk
ISBN 0-333-40225-1 Pbk export

CONTENTS

General editor's preface   vii

Acknowledgements   ix

1 **Life and background**   1.1   Early years   1
                               1.2   Plays before the First
                                     World War   2
                               1.3   1914–1923   3
                               1.4   *Saint Joan*   4
                               1.5   Shaw after *Saint Joan*   4

2 **Plot synopsis and critical
   commentary**   7

3 **Themes and issues**   3.1   Joan of Arc: the historical
                                     figure   33
                               3.2   Shaw's sources   34
                               3.3   Shaw's nineteenth-century
                                     predecessors   36
                               3.4   Shaw and history   38
                               3.5   Joan as a revolutionary
                                     heroine   40
                               3.6   The waning of the Middle
                                     Ages   42
                               3.7   Joan as a bourgeoise   43
                               3.8   Joan as a feminist   44
                               3.9   Joan and creative evolution   45
                               3.10 Shaw and Joan's 'voices'   46
                               3.11 Joan and Christ   49

4 **Technical features**   4.1   The structure of the play   51
                               4.2   *Saint Joan* as tragedy   53
                               4.3   Characterisation   55
                               4.4   Rhetoric and debate   58
                               4.5   Humour   59
                               4.6   Stage directions   61

5 **Critical analysis of a
   selected passage**   5.1   Passage   63
                               5.2   Commentary   65

6 **Critical reception**   6.1   The early reviews and
                                      commentaries   69
                                6.2   Later standing of *Saint Joan* 72

Revision Questions   73
Further reading   75

GENERAL EDITOR'S PREFACE

The aim of the Macmillan Master Guides is to help you to appreciate the
book you are studying by providing information about it and by suggesting ways of reading and thinking about it which will lead to a fuller
understanding. The section on the writer's life and background has been
designed to illustrate those aspects of the writer's life which have
influenced the work, and to place it in its personal and literary context.
The summaries and critical commentary are of special importance in
that each brief summary of the action is followed by an examination of
the significant critical points. The space which might have been given
to repetitive explanatory notes has been devoted to a detailed analysis
of the kind of passage which might confront you in an examination.
Literary criticism is concerned with both the broader aspects of the
work being studied and with its detail. The ideas which meet us in
reading a great work of literature, and their relevance to us today, are
an essential part of our study, and our Guides look at the thought of
their subject in some detail. But just as essential is the craft with which
the writer has constructed his work of art, and this is considered under
several technical headings — characterisation, language, style and stage-
craft.

The authors of these Guides are all teachers and writers of wide
experience, and they have chosen to write about books they admire and
know well in the belief that they can communicate their admiration to
you. But you yourself must read and know intimately the book you are
studying. No one can do that for you. You should see this book as a
lamp-post. Use it to shed light, not to lean against. If you know your
text and know what it is saying about life, and how it says it, then you
will enjoy it, and there is no better way of passing an examination in
literature.

JAMES GIBSON

ACKNOWLEDGEMENTS

The author and publishers wish to thank the Society of Authors on behalf of the Bernard Shaw Estate for extracts from *Saint Joan* by G. B. Shaw. The cover illustration shows *Joan of Arc kissing the Sword of Deliverance* by Dante Gabriel Rossetti © Christies, London, and is reproduced by courtesy of the Bridgeman Art Library.

I owe a special debt to my husband, Richard, both for his interest in the project, and for making it possible for me to complete it.

LEONÉE ORMOND

1 LIFE AND BACKGROUND

1.1 EARLY YEARS

George Bernard Shaw was born in Dublin in 1856, the third child of an improvident corn-broker, George Carr Shaw, and of his musical wife, Lucinda. The boy was educated at the Wesleyan Connection College in Dublin, an experience which left him with a life-long scorn for formal education.

The true story of Bernard Shaw's early years will probably only emerge with the publication of Michael Holroyd's official biography. The existing biographies are based upon a version of his background provided by Shaw himself. From the available evidence, it is clear that the Shaw home was not a relaxed or warm one, and that the boy's parents were ill-suited to one another. He found relief in music, compulsive reading, and in studying the paintings in the National Gallery of Ireland.

In 1873, Mrs Shaw settled in London, where she established a career as a teacher of singing. Her two daughters went with her, and Bernard was left behind with his father. In 1871 he had begun work as a clerk in an estate agent's office, eventually rising to the position of cashier. Life with his father was depressing, and it was with relief that Shaw left Dublin and joined his mother in London in 1876, intending to establish himself as a writer. He earned a little through intermittent journalism and occasional office jobs, while writing five novels. Four were published in the 1880s, two of them serially, but attracted limited notice.

During his lean years in London, Shaw espoused a number of political and social causes. He became a vegetarian, and joined the socialist Fabian Society shortly after its foundation in 1884. Throughout his long life, his energy was formidable. He was continuously occupied with causes which engaged his attention. His passionate intellectual honesty and witty iconoclasm made him a well-known spokesman on numerous issues. Shaw trained himself to be a fine public speaker, and was a member of the St Pancras Vestry (later Borough Council) from 1897 to 1903. His studies in Marxist theory influenced the way he presented social conflict in his plays, and have an influence on some of the themes presented in *Saint Joan*.

At the outset, Shaw was inclined to see the theatre as only an extension of this, as an effective way of propagating his ideas and of hastening reform. His brilliant theatre criticism, however, suggests that this was not the whole story, and his own plays would surely not continue to draw audiences were he no more than a commentator.

1.2 PLAYS BEFORE THE FIRST WORLD WAR

Shaw's earliest plays exemplify his admiration for the work of the Norwegian dramatist, Henrik Ibsen (1828–1906), about whom he wrote an important critical work, *The Quintessence of Ibsenism* (1891). Ibsen's major plays were revolutionary in their depiction of a modern middle-class setting, and in their discussion of contemporary issues. The younger author followed him in both respects. *Widowers' Houses* (1892) takes up the subject of slum landlords, and *Mrs Warren's Profession* (1893) is concerned with prostitution.

Shaw's plays are difficult to categorise. They vary considerably in subject matter, but share a common impulse to arouse interest and to provoke the audience to think by disappointing and overturning their expectations. He resisted the traditions of romantic drama and remorselessly set them on their head as he probed economic, sexual and theatrical conventions.

Of Shaw's early plays, *Arms and the Man* of 1894 is probably the most often performed. Here the heroine, Raina, rejects her heroic suitor, who has distinguished himself in battle, for the rational and utterly unromantic deserter who climbs into her bedroom. The outcome reversed all the cherished beliefs of late nineteenth-century audiences. In *Man and Superman* (1903) another convention was outraged when the rationalist, Jack Tanner, is pursued by the heroine Ann Whitefield. Shaw represents Ann as the agent of what he calls the Life Force, a power intent upon moving man towards perfection by producing a child, a potential superman. Joan's aims are apparently very different from those of Ann Whitefield but she too is seen as a powerful agent of the Life Force.

Between 1904 and 1907, Shaw was closely associated with the Royal Court Theatre in London, then under the management of J. E. Vedrenne (1867–1930) and Harley Granville Barker (1877–1946). Their preference for radical modern drama gave Shaw his chance, and eleven of his plays were performed there, among them *John Bull's Other Island* (1904) and *Major Barbara* (1905). In *Major Barbara* Shaw explored and attacked the demoralising effects of charitable institutions like the Salvation Army, putting forward a case for the building up of efficient and powerful industries. In a play which explores the limitations of the Christian way of life, Shaw deliberately parallels his heroine, Barbara Undershaft, with Christ. This represents an important analogy with *Saint Joan*, another profound exploration of a female protagonist.

Androcles and the Lion (1912) deals with the Roman persecution of the Christians, and continues the discussion of themes of Christianity and martyrdom, although the threatened martyrdom is avoided, and the general effect is that of comedy. Like the condemned Christians in *Androcles*, Joan is faced with choices which may lead to martyrdom, a subject which Shaw discusses at length in the Preface to *Androcles* (1915).

1.3 **1914–1923**

Shortly before the First World War, Shaw achieved a considerable critical and public success with his play about a flower girl and a professor of phonetics, *Pygmalion*. The outbreak of war, however resulted in a relatively unproductive period. Shaw's criticisms of the conduct of the war were construed as unpatriotic and his two major post-war plays, *Heartbreak House* (1920) and the five-play cycle, *Back to Methuselah* (1922), were not received with enthusiasm. *Heartbreak House*, like other Shaw plays, argues that capitalism is analogous with theft, and declares that a combination of a misguided and mediocre government, and an inactive educated class can drive the country onto the rocks of disaster. The more visionary *Back to Methuselah* advocates a redemption of society through the extension of the life-span of certain gifted and visionary individuals. Shaw himself believed these two plays to be his finest, but contemporary audiences and critics found them

4

long, tedious and undramatic. They were seen as platforms for Shaw's political and social theories, theories with which few of his audience were in sympathy.

1.4 *SAINT JOAN*

It was against this unpromising background that Shaw, now a man in his middle sixties, began work on *Saint Joan*. As early as 1913, he had told the actress, Mrs Patrick Campbell, that he would like to write a play about Joan of Arc, but he was slow to approach the task. It is said that Shaw's wife, Charlotte, a wealthy Anglo-Irish woman whom he married in 1898, encouraged him by leaving books on Joan lying around their house. One of these was T. Douglas Murray's translation of the manuscripts of the trial of Joan of Arc, lent to Shaw by Sydney Cockerell, keeper of the Fitzwilliam Museum in Cambridge.

One important stimulus came in 1920, with the canonisation of Joan by the Roman Catholic Church. Another was the actress Sybil Thorndike's performance in a revival of P. B. Shelley's (1792-1822) historical drama, *The Cenci*. Beatrice Cenci was involved in the murder of the father who had raped her, and *The Cenci*, like *Saint Joan*, ends with the heroine's execution.

Shaw wrote *Saint Joan* in six months, and the first performance was given at the Garrick Theatre, New York on 28 December 1923 by the New York Theatre Guild, with Winifred Lenihan in the leading role. Sybil Thorndike opened in the play at the New Theatre, London on 26 March 1925.

1.5 SHAW AFTER *SAINT JOAN*

Saint Joan was probably Shaw's most successful play, and many regard it as his masterpiece. The award of the Nobel Prize for literature in 1926 was generally seen as a tribute to the author of *Saint Joan*.

The Malvern Festival, founded by Sir Barry Jackson (1879-1961) in 1929, provided a setting for the revival of twenty of Shaw's plays. Some, including *The Apple Cart* (1929) and *In Good King Charles's Golden Days* 1939) had their first British production there. His work reached an even wider audience when several of his plays were filmed, among them *Pygmalion*, *Major Barbara* and *Caesar and Cleopatra*.

The dramatist lived for another twenty-seven years after *Saint Joan*, dying at the age of ninety-four. He continued writing plays until 1950. Action is at a minimum in these late works. The strain of fantasy becomes more pronounced, and discussion and analysis are even more dominant than before. These late plays can be highly effective, but probably few would disagree that *Saint Joan* marks a high point which Shaw never quite achieved again.

2 PLOT SYNOPSIS AND CRITICAL COMMENTARY

2.1 SCENE ONE

Synopsis

When the first scene opens, Robert de Baudricourt, Squire of
Vaucouleurs, is on the stage with his steward. De Baudricourt is complaining bitterly that there are no eggs, and the steward is assuring him
that there will be none until de Baudricourt gives his support to Joan,
who is waiting outside.

Joan, on her entry, asks de Baudricourt to equip her to ride to
Chinon, so that she can persuade the Dauphin to give her an army to
raise the English siege of Orléans. One of the fighting men attached
to the castle, Bertrand de Poulengey, explains to de Baudricourt that
Joan's inspiration and strength of purpose may be an asset to the hard-
pressed French. De Poulengey, with a handful of soldiers, is prepared
to accompany Joan to Chinon.

The blustering de Baudricourt, persuaded by de Poulengey's arguments, and overwhelmed by Joan's determination, gives his permission
for the expedition. After Joan's departure, the steward announces that
the hens have laid five dozen eggs.

Commentary

The opening scene of *Saint Joan* represents the first round of Joan's
fight to free France from an alien rule. Her opponent here, Robert
de Baudricourt, is a weak man. For all his noisy protestations, he can
put up little resistance to her determined assaults. The tension of the
scene relates to this struggle for dominance, the outcome of which is

never seriously in doubt. Shaw, characteristically, spins it out with a good deal of farcical comedy.

With the single exception of Scene Six, Shaw begins each scene of *Saint Joan* with figures already placed upon the stage. Scene One opens in the middle of de Baudricourt's harangue to his steward. With the abruptness of a film camera, Shaw brings up the lights on the Squire's dramatic, but at first unexplained, explosion of rage: 'No eggs! No eggs!! Thousand thunders, man, what do you mean by no eggs?' The servile steward has to endure his master's bullying, because the hens do not lay, nor do the cows give milk. The hens dominate the beginning and end of the scene. In the penultimate line we are reminded of them again when the steward rushes in to tell de Baudricourt: 'The hens are laying like mad, sir. Five dozen eggs!' The miracle of the eggs was Shaw's own invention, a substitute for the actual 'miracle' which he believed had convinced de Baudricourt, Joan's news of a French defeat at the Battle of Herrings.

Miraculous egg-laying is appropriate to the domestic imagery of this first scene. De Baudricourt mockingly asks his steward whether he, de Baudricourt, is squire of Vaucouleurs, or a cowboy. Later he tells Joan 'I suppose you think raising a siege is as easy as chasing a cow out of a meadow'. Joan herself responds in kind, assuring de Baudricourt that French soldiers will one day 'drive the poor goddams before them like sheep'. Such comparisons are fitting to the early part of the play, when the heroine's life as a country girl is no more than a few days behind her.

Much of the comedy of this first scene comes from de Baudricourt's bluster. Try as he will to act the strong man, he is unable to influence the course of events. Shaw's stage directions show that he wanted the part to be played with broad humour. After Joan's first entrance, de Baudricourt 'feeling that he has lost ground, brings down his two fists squarely on the table, and inflates his chest imposingly to cure the unwelcome and only too familiar sensation'. De Baudricourt indulges in an unproductive verbal attack on his steward, an obvious social inferior, firing questions and accusing him with mounting derision of being 'the worst, most incompetent, drivelling snivelling jibbering jabbering idiot of a steward in France'.

When de Baudricourt turns his jibes on Joan, the force of her single-mindedness renders her invulnerable. She makes two entrances, first after de Baudricourt's attack on the steward, and then again after the very different confidential discussion between de Baudricourt and

Poulengey. On both occasions, Joan seizes the initiative and enters as though refusal of her demands were impossible. Her practical grasp of what is needed for her proposed journey contrasts effectively with de Baudricourt's manipulation of empty language. When he tells Joan that he is going to assert himself, she undercuts him by saying: 'Please do, squire', and then gives him a list of what she wants. Joan is unconscious of any need to do battle with her feudal lord. She behaves with the greatest politeness, and meets his oaths with 'unruffled sweetness'. To his 'Well, I am damned', she provides a literal response: 'No, squire: God is very merciful'. De Baudricourt's frustrated threat to throw the steward down the stairs, and his suggestion that Joan be taken home and thrashed, reveal him for what he is, a straightforward bully, unable to conceive of any solution beyond brute force.

The first scene is important in establishing Joan's character, her simplicity, her strength and her unblinking optimism. It also serves to open up the historical background to the story. In his appeal to de Baudricourt, Poulengey sets out the military situation, ostensibly as part of his argument, but in fact for the benefit of the audience. By this means, Shaw explains the relative position of the French and English armies and the doubtful status of the French Dauphin until the coronation takes place.

Scene One is a good illustration of the way Shaw translates original source material into drama. He conflates Joan's three meetings with de Baudricourt into one, and introduces a number of telling details from Douglas Murray's *Jeanne D'Arc*. This transcript of Joan's trial and rehabilitation provided Shaw with such details as the names of her companions on the road to Chinon, the red colour of her dress, and the cost of her horse, sixteen francs. From the same source came de Baudricourt's taunt that Joan should be taken home and her ears boxed, as well as the information that Jean de Metz gave her the money with which she provided alms for the poor. In the account which Bertrand de Poulengey gave to the enquiry of 1455, he reported that de Baudricourt had asked Joan: 'Who is this Lord of whom you speak?', and that Joan had replied 'The King of Heaven', lines which Shaw uses almost unchanged. He does the same with de Baudricourt's parting injunction to Joan: 'Then let come what may: I can do no more.'

For all its comedy, the first scene contains both ironic and direct hints of the serious issues of the play. In the opening lines, de Baudricourt tells his steward that he 'burns witches', and he counters the steward's assertion that the lack of eggs is 'the act of God', with a warning against blaming 'your Maker'. Joan, who sees everything as an act of God, immediately declares her special and direct relationship with Him, the very thing which will bring her to the stake.

De Baudricourt's coarse comments on girls who talk to soldiers, and his assumption that de Poulengey's interest in Joan is a sexual one, are, on one level, comic indications of his failure of understanding; on another, they are early statements of a favourite Shavian theme, that the true genius will not become trammelled in sexuality. De Baudricourt's misunderstanding draws from de Poulengey the assertion that Joan is set apart: 'I should as soon think of the Blessed Virgin herself in that way, as of this girl.'

Shaw is often accused of unnecessary prolixity in his plays, but the opening scenes of *Saint Joan* are by contrast taut and spare. Almost everything said between Joan, de Poulengey and de Baudricourt relates to Shaw's central intentions. De Baudricourt's warning to de Poulengey that Joan is not a peasant but a bourgeoise states the theme of emergent individualism. The members of the rising middle-class, no longer impoverished and uneducated vassals, would think for themselves and make their own decisions. Joan herself raises the nationalist issue, telling de Baudricourt that the English should stay in England, speak their own language, and not invade another country. De Baudricourt, in his reply, prefigures Warwick in Scene Four in his support for the feudal system, and in his denial that national divisions, as opposed to feudal ones, have any validity. Joan's argument is that his duty is to God and not to his feudal lord.

Even the moment of glorious comedy when de Baudricourt looks for his halo is a play on the nature of sanctity. The whole dialogue between Joan and de Baudricourt ironically juxtaposes the Christian platitudes of someone essentially worldly with the straightforward religious beliefs of the saint: a theme which Shaw continues to state until the very last line of the play.

2.2 SCENE TWO

Synopsis

In the castle of Chinon, the Lord Chamberlain and Commander of the army, the Duke de la Trémouille, is awaiting the arrival of the Dauphin with the Archbishop of Rheims. Gilles de Rais (Bluebeard) enters, and tells them of the death of Foul Mouthed Frank, a soldier well known for his violent oaths. Frank was drowned after being warned against swearing when at the point of death. Captain La Hire confirms the story, and makes it clear to the audience that it was Joan who administered the rebuke.

When the Dauphin appears, the Archbishop and Lord Chamberlain treat him with scorn, throwing doubt on his legitimacy. He counters by reminding de la Trémouille of France's desperate military position, and by announcing that de Baudricourt is sending him his own saint. Both the Archbishop and the Chamberlain tell him that Joan must not be admitted, but they finally persuade themselves that she can do no harm. In a private discussion between them on the subject of miracles, the Archbishop assures the Chamberlain that miracles must be judged by their effect, not by any appeal to supernatural causes.

The courtiers test Joan by telling her that Gilles de Rais is the Dauphin, but she recognises the trick at once. Alone with the Dauphin, Joan declares that, however little his inclination, he must fight for his kingdom, and that he will never be taken seriously until he is crowned. In the end, the Dauphin is persuaded by Joan's eloquence to give her command of the army with the object of raising the siege of Orléans. De la Trémouille is furious, but the rest of the court proclaim their determination to set out to save Orléans.

Commentary

Scene Two of *Saint Joan* is in many ways a pendant to Scene One. Joan's triumph in her local castle of Vaucouleurs is here repeated in the Dauphin's court at Chinon. The effect of Joan's strength of character, and the desperation of those in authority, combine to give her success, a success in which inertia and opportunism play a large part. Where in Scene One de Baudricourt concludes: 'This may be all rot, Polly; but the troops might swallow it, though nothing that we can say seems able to put any fight into them'; here, in Scene Two, La Trémouille tells the Archbishop: 'Oh, let them have their way. Dunois' men will give up the town in spite of him if somebody does not put fresh spunk into them.'

In Scene One, Shaw uses the device, particularly effective in Ibsen's *Hedda Gabler*, of delaying the entry of the title character, and so whetting the audience's curiosity. In the second scene, Shaw extends this tension for even longer. It is not until more than half-way through the action, when the rights and wrongs of her cause have been extensively canvassed by leading members of the court, that Joan herself appears, dressed in male attire. The impact of her entry is greatly increased by the stage setting. The earlier part of the scene is played before curtains, which are then drawn open to reveal the full depth of the stage. The sense of surrounding closet intrigue, entirely alien to Joan's openness and honesty, is greatly increased by this simple change of set.

Dress and appearance are also used to good effect. Several characters (including Charles himself) comment on the Dauphin's unkingly appearance, which parallels his unkingly status. His courtiers are smartly dressed and he appears among them as the meanest of all. Joan, in trying to persuade him to buy new clothes, is also trying to make him perform his role properly. Joan herself is dressed for the part she has come to perform, but she too attracts ridicule from those more concerned with surface than with function. In her view, a king should look like a king, a soldier like a soldier.

The movement of the scene follows a similar pattern to the first. The dialogues between the Archbishop and la Trémouille and between the Dauphin and Joan contain the most important matter, and these are juxtaposed, as in the first scene, with passages where a large number of characters are present. Both scenes lead to a triumphant conclusion for the heroine. Here, in the most conventionally theatrical moment of the play, the court shouts 'To Orleans!', the Archbishop gives his blessing and Joan falls to her knees.

As in the previous scene, Joan must win over the doubtful, but in the Dauphin she finds an opponent very different from de Baudricourt. Charles has no *amour propre*, and makes no attempt to live up to an inflated image of himself. Instead, his throw-away manner conceals considerable intelligence. He tells Joan: 'These fighting fellows lose all on the treaties that they gain on the fights. If we can only have a treaty, the English are sure to have the worst of it, because they are better at fighting than at thinking'. Joan cannot simply talk across this, as she did in the first scene. She has to pit her will-power and her common sense against the Dauphin's cynicism: 'If the English win, it is they that will make the treaty; and then God help poor France'.

Shaw himself may have had considerable sympathy with the Dauphin's case. In his early play, *Arms and the Man*, the heroine, given the choice between two lovers, rejects the dashing soldier for the quiet man of business. To win the Dauphin over, Joan has to persuade him that he cannot simply remain in his present position, and to rouse him to action. The rhythm of her prose, together with her choice of words, echoes the language of the Bible, as Joan prophesies a glorious future, and then concludes with a rhetorical question: 'Wilt be a poor little Judas, and betray me and Him that sent me?'

While the movement of Scene Two looks back to the play's opening, the two conversations between the Archbishop and the Lord Chamberlain lead directly into those in Scene Four between Bishop Cauchon and the Earl of Warwick, their Anglo-Burgundian equivalents. The French pair in Scene Two, a 'full-fed political prelate', and a 'monstrous arrogant wineskin', are particularly unappealing. La Trémouille is a caricature general, probably reflecting Shaw's contempt for the generals of his own time. If the Archbishop has a more subtle mind, his cynical worldliness betrays his calling. Like Cauchon, he is entirely committed to upholding the Church's role as an organisation with total responsibility for man's spiritual welfare, less concerned with the message of God than with the Church militant on earth.

Throughout the play Joan is to be crushed between the millstones of the Church and the military. In this scene, Church temporarily sides with her, won over by her sincerity, and by her possible usefulness. La Trémouille is never drawn to her side, and stands threateningly apart from the triumphant conclusion. This pattern is again repeated in Scene Four and in the trial Scene. Cauchon tries to save her soul, but Warwick is inexorably bent on her destruction.

The ending, however perilously achieved, gives this second scene the traditional form of comedy. The heroine carries the day, if only in the flawed context of the court at Chinon. This is the most ill-conducted of courts, where a page has to shout more than once in order to make an announcement, and where the Dauphin carries on a childish running battle with his advisers. The game in which Joan has to 'spot the Dauphin' loses its well-tried quality as part of a folk-tale, and becomes instead a device to ward off encroaching boredom. The fact that Gilles de Rais, better known as the mass-murderer Bluebeard, plays the Dauphin's part, gives an additional level of artifice to the whole episode. This is not Victorian costume drama, but a satirical account of court-life, where Joan's simplicity stands out in sharp relief.

2.3 SCENE THREE

Synopsis
Dunois, the Bastard of Orléans, is standing by the Loire outside Orléans,

urging the wind to change so that he can cross the river and launch an attack on the English who are besieging the town. He and his page see a kingfisher and delight in its beauty. Joan rushes in complaining that she has been led to the wrong side of the river, and demanding that they attack Orléans at once. Dunois explains that unless the wind changes he cannot take his men upstream and attack the English from the rear. Nothing can be achieved by assaulting the bridgehead as Joan wishes. Dunois hopes that Joan will achieve a miracle, and is just taking her to church to pray for one when the wind does, indeed, change. As the page points this out, they at first suppose that he has seen another kingfisher. Then, overcome by emotion, Dunois offers Joan his commander's baton and they set out together to raise the siege.

Commentary

The third scene forms a brief prologue to Joan's greatest military victory, the raising of the siege of Orléans. For the last time, Shaw uses the upward pattern of the first and second scenes. Two characters, Dunois and his page, speak of her, and, as before, Joan follows her entry by winning over a doubting ally. This time her weapon is not her eloquence, to which Dunois is immune, but a miracle.

The brevity of the scene has disturbed some critics, while others have been puzzled by the uncharacteristic lyricism of its opening passage. Shaw here approximates more closely to the complex religious symbolism of the middle ages than in any other part of the play. Dunois' attempt at a poem, and his joy in the passing kingfisher, suggest different aspects of femininity. For him, the wind is 'wanton', 'womanish', 'strumpet', and 'harlot', whereas the blue bird, the kingfisher, recalls the archetypal virginity of the Virgin, a figure readily associated with Joan herself. The swift passage of the bird as Dunois is awaiting Joan prefigures her entry in shining armour.

Shaw's choice of the kingfisher, or halcyon, a bird traditionally associated with charms to make the wind change, introduces another kind of symbolism, drawn from classical rather than Christian sources. In the classical legend, the grief-stricken Alcyone, finding the drowned body of her husband, Ceyx, threw herself into the sea. The gods changed both husband and wife into kingfishers, birds which became emblems of fine weather in the classical world.

This sensitive passage is followed by one of Shaw's most earthy dialogues, as Dunois explains military technicalities to the hot-headed Joan. The central dichotomy of Church and army is again marked by

Dunois' words: 'You are in love with war', where, as Joan at once recalls, the Archbishop in Scene Two had told her that she was 'in love with religion'. Dunois follows with the statement: 'I welcome you as a saint, not as a soldier'. The ensuing battle is indeed won by Joan, but the soldiers set out before she does, and Shaw, like Dunois, implies that her real function here is to give inspiration, not to usurp Dunois' role as a commander.

2.4 SCENE FOUR

Synopsis

Scene Four is set in the English camp, on the occasion of a visit to the English leader, the Earl of Warwick, from the Bishop of Beauvais, Pierre Cauchon. The meeting has been arranged so that they can devise a policy to destroy Joan.

A third character in the scene is an English chaplain, John de Stogumber, who is attached to the Cardinal of Winchester, great-uncle to the young king Henry VI.

At the opening, Warwick is reading, while de Stogumber tries to interest him in the military situation. The dialogue between Warwick and de Stogumber, before the entry of Cauchon, tells of events since the third scene. Joan has not only raised the siege of Orléans, but has won further victories. De Stogumber insists that such English defeats must require a supernatural explanation, and that Joan must be a witch. Warwick gives measured answers to each of de Stogumber's outbursts. Like Dunois in the previous scene, he refuses to discount military professionalism, believing that Dunois' skill, rather than Joan's possibly supernatural powers, are responsible for the change in fortune.

Warwick questions de Stogumber's description of himself as an 'Englishman', so restating the theme of emergent nationalism and its possible effect on feudalism and on the Church, first raised by de Baudricourt in the first scene.

The entry of the Bishop of Beauvais begins a verbal battle between Church and state. He and Warwick open with a formal exchange of courtesies, followed by Warwick's statement that Joan is about to crown the Dauphin at Rheims, and that the English army is powerless to prevent it.

Warwick's aim is to persuade Cauchon to agree to condemn Joan to death as soon as she is bought or captured. True to Shaw's conception of Cauchon as a sincere Churchman, the Bishop refuses to prejudge the issue. The impetuous de Stogumber undermines Warwick's diplomatic approach by emphasising the case intemperately. He annoys the Bishop, who tells him sharply that the defeat of an English army is not an infallible sign of sorcery. Though Cauchon has sided with the Anglo-Burgundian party in the conflict, he recognises the incompetence of the English captains, Talbot and Glasdale, who have been captured and killed respectively. Cauchon nearly storms out of the tent when de Stogumber calls him a traitor, a crisis which Warwick smoothly resolves by explaining that in England treachery means opposition to English interests, not the betrayal of lord or friend.

Cauchon forcefully states his duty as a Churchman to achieve Joan's salvation, not burn her out of hand to please the English. Warwick begins to fear that Cauchon will not help him, but, to Warwick's relief, Cauchon agrees that the devil probably has Joan in his power. He insists, however, that Joan is a heretic, not a witch; and, in the passage which follows, he makes out a case for the Church, explaining that Joan's heresy is a matter of far more importance to him than her military victories.

The Bishop argues that Joan is an instrument of the devil's design to take over all human souls. Her crime is that she does not approach God through the Church, but directly in her own person. He compares her to two Christian reformers, Johan Hus and John Wyclif, as well as Muhammad, the founder of Islam, whose early career Cauchon sees as analogous to Joan's. The Bishop prophesies chaos and damnation if the practice of approaching God directly should become universal.

Warwick greets Cauchon's impassioned arguments cooly. Having travelled in the Holy Land, his attitude to Islam is far more tolerant, and he doubts whether Joan plans to overthrow the Church at all. Warwick's anxiety is aroused by another of Joan's assertions: that a king should devote his kingdom to God, and be himself God's regent on earth. Warwick sees this as an attack on the feudal system, which would result in a shift of power from the nobles to the king.

Cauchon is as cool about Warwick's political arguments as Warwick was about his religious ones. Most kings are poor statesmen, and will need advisers, he says, but Warwick tartly responds that such advisers may be Churchmen.

At this low point in their discussion, Cauchon diplomatically suggests that they abandon dissension and work together towards the defeat of Joan. In agreeing to this, Warwick draws an analogy between Joan's dual conception of Church and state. She is championing the individual's right to approach God without intermediaries, whether Churchmen or nobles. Inventing a new word, he calls this 'Protestantism', the protest of the individual against Church interference. Cauchon responds by devising another word, 'Nationalism', a term to express his fear that the separate identity of nations may one day cut across the universalising theories of Christendom. Without Christian unity he foresees a world plunged into continuous war.

To these concepts, de Stogumber can only respond with a simple statement that Joan is a rebel against her own sex, the Church and God. Above all, she is fighting against England, and for this reason she must be destroyed.

At the end of the scene, Cauchon and Warwick seal their uneasy compact, with Cauchon still insisting that he will try to save Joan's soul. De Stogumber gives vent to fresh spleen, and the Bishop ironically blesses him for his simplicity. The scene concludes in a manner particularly ominous for Joan.

Commentary

Scene Four differs markedly from the others for a number of reasons. It is the only scene from which Joan is absent, and, with the exception of the Epilogue, it has least foundation in historical fact. Most important of all, it is almost entirely static. Apart from the entry and exit of Cauchon, the characters only move when they stand up, whether in anger or in greeting, before resuming their seats. Such limited action means that there is nothing to watch except the play of facial expression. The audience's attention is entirely concentrated on the issues raised. The trial scene is similarly sedentary, but there are far more characters, and, because Joan's life is at risk, the audience's emotions are more deeply involved.

This scene also breaks decisively from those which precede it in its introduction of three new characters, none of whom has yet appeared in the play. This is appropriate to the argument, which introduces new and provocative ideas about the historical role of Joan of Arc. The theories under discussion are by no means easy for an audience to grasp. Shaw here puts his ability to sustain enthralling intellectual dialogue to a severe test. Shaw himself regarded this scene as the beginning of the 'real play', describing the earlier episodes as 'flapdoodles'.

Given these limitations, the playwright brilliantly succeeds in rendering this scene dramatic, by contrasting three vivid characters who are representatives of opposing points of view. Warwick is worldly, urbane, and highly intelligent; under a smooth facade, he ruthlessly manipulates the discussion for his own ends. Cauchon, as becomes a Churchman, is inclined to preach. His impressive speeches are marked by rhetoric and Latinate prose. He appears more sincere than Warwick, but he is also revealed as a fanatic ecclesiastical conservative. Warwick, with his liberal defence of Jews and Muhammadans, his love of books, is the more attractive character of the two.

Shaw was wise to introduce a third figure, John de Stogumber, to counteract the clash between Warwick and Cauchon. His behaviour throughout the scene is typical of a pig-headed Englishman, a type whom Shaw much enjoyed satirising. If his companions are severally capable of liberalism and vision, de Stogumber represents the attitude of Joan's humbler opponents, who traduced her as a witch and a harlot. His version is not unlike Shakespeare's in *Henry VI*. De Stogumber's major function in this scene is to enliven the discussion between Cauchon and Warwick, punctuating their presentation of large and complex issues with expressions of uncomprehending wrath. The audience feels considerable tension in anticipation of de Stogumber's next outburst. When he calls Cauchon a traitor, the discussion all but flares into acrimony, and this threat is present throughout the scene. De Stogumber's folly provides much of the comedy, provoking laughter even when he is exaggerating the audience's own prejudices. Some of his assertions verge on the absurd, and it could be argued that Shaw goes too far in placing such a caricature in a serious context.

The dialogue between Warwick and Cauchon centres on their presentation of the separate arguments in favour of the Church and the aristocracy. When Cauchon gives his account of his reasons for wishing to be rid of Joan, Warwick balances it with a statement of his own. Neither listens very attentively to the other. The discovery of the new terms Protestantism and Nationalism provides a verbal summation of their earlier statements. It also establishes their community of interest as both contribute to the discovery of words, familiar enough to the audience, but supposedly new to the characters. The whole scene, with its concerted chorus of threats, casts a shadow over Joan's triumph at Rheims, on the aftermath of which the fifth scene will open.

2.5 SCENE FIVE

Synopsis

Scene Five is set in Rheims Cathedral, where the coronation of the Dauphin as Charles VII has just taken place. At the opening of the scene, Joan is kneeling before a station of the cross (a sculptured group representing one of the stages of Christ's progress to His crufixion). Dunois enters and tries to persuade her to go out into the town to receive the homage of the people. Joan refuses to distract attention from the new king.

When Dunois recalls the battle for Orléans, Joan regrets the dullness of life without fighting. Dunois reminds her that fighting, like other pleasures, has to be rationed. He sadly warns Joan that she has made enemies of courtiers, Churchmen and military leaders, all jealous of her success. In her simplicity, Joan cannot understand why her actions have given rise to hatred, not to gratitude. Joan declares that she will go home after taking Paris, but Dunois ominously hints that she will not be allowed to take the capital.

Joan confides to Dunois that she hears her voices in the sound of church bells, but Dunois angers her by refusing to believe in her voices. in a sudden change of mood, Joan expresses her affection for him.

The king enters, complaining bitterly and ungratefully about the discomforts of his coronation. Joan, shaken by her conversation with Dunois, tells Charles that she is planning to go home. King and courtiers are openly relieved at the idea of her departure, but, when La Hire and Dunois begin to recall the fights in which they have all taken part, Joan suddenly asks Dunois whether they might take Paris first. The King, horrified, prefers to arrange a treaty - an idea which appals Joan. She incurs the wrath of the Archbishop, who accuses her of spiritual pride. Joan's reaction is to claim superiority of judgement, since hers expresses the voice of God. She demands that the French continue to attack, but Dunois recommends prudence, accusing Joan of taking no notice of essential military practicalities. Dunois warns her that, once captured, she would be useless to the French army, and so not worth rescuing. Charles says that he could not afford a ransom, and the Archbishop, arguing that she has scorned the Church, also denies her his support. Dunois specifically cautions her against trying to raise the siege of Compiègne. Joan, refusing to heed their warnings, commends herself to God. She declares that there is strength in isolation, and leaves them as she goes outside to the crowd. In a brief passage after her departure, each remaining character expresses his feelings about her, Dunois and the Archbishop reiterating their belief that her doom is imminent.

Commentary

Scene Five is anti-climactic in mood, and difficult to play in the theatre. Shaw avoids presenting the coronation itself, and the King's account of it is a further blow to romantic expectations. Joan has achieved her objective and crowned the King. That done, the sense of triumph is temporarily dissipated. The next step is uncertain. Joan believes that military success must be followed up at all costs, others would prefer to make peace. Everybody wishes that Joan would go home.

One problem with the scene is its predictability. There is a certain warmth and intimacy in Joan's opening dialogue with Dunois, but the passage with King and courtiers which follows presents an almost stylised chorus of prophecy and disaster. With the benefit of hindsight, Shaw makes his characters warn Joan of the way in which she will be captured at Compiègne, and of how she will be abandoned by her own side. Shaw uses these warnings to prefigure coming events which will take place before the opening of the trial scene.

Joan herself is somewhat unsympathetic. The audience can understand her frustration, but her uncompromising stridency confirms the pride of which the Archbishop warns her. There is a strong suggestion that pride is the tragic flaw in her character which will bring about her destruction.

Certain themes from Scene Four are carried on here. Dunois puts the case for the army, as did Warwick, while the Archbishop's argument that Joan has refused to bow to the Church, and has addressed herself directly to God, is a simpler reflection of Cauchon's statements in Scenes Four and Six. It underlines the point that Joan is opposing herself to all entrenched interests, whether French or Anglo-Burgundian.

2.6 SCENE SIX

Synopsis

The setting for Joan's trial is in a hall of Rouen Castle. Warwick enters, intent on speaking with Cauchon before the proceedings commence. Cauchon brings with him the Inquisitor, John Lemaître, and the Promoter (prosecutor) John D'Estivet. Warwick emphasises his impatience with the slowness of the legal process, and demands to know when Joan's trial will end. The Inquisitor replies that the court has so far been concerned only with preliminaries, but that the trial itself is now about to begin. Having thought Joan a political prisoner, he has now decided that there is a case of heresy to answer. To Warwick's underlying demands that Joan should be condemned forthwith, Cauchon and D'Estivet respond with strong statements that their intention is to save Joan, should that prove possible. The Inquisitor cuts short Warwick's threats to act without the Church, by telling him that Joan is apparently determined to condemn herself through her own evidence.

As soon as the court assembles, de Stogumber, associating himself with Canon de Courcelles, complains bitterly that the number of charges against Joan has been drastically reduced, and that laboriously collected evidence is being disregarded. The Inquisitor confesses to taking this step. He fears that, if the court's time is taken up with minor matters like the supposed theft of the Bishop of Senlis' horse, the central issue of heresy may be evaded.

Brother Martin Ladvenu asks the Inquisitor whether Joan's apparently heretical statements are any more than the expressions of simple faith. The Inquisitor responds by stating that most heretics begin as men and women of exceptional piety. Extreme religious experience can lead to unnatural behaviour and to sexual licence and perversion. Those who put their own judgement before that of the Church, are not liars but self-deceivers. They honestly believe that they are following the dictates of God.

The Inquisitor tells the court that they must harden their hearts. Joan does not look like a sinner and English assertions that she is unchaste can be disregarded. Spiritual pride co-exists in her with profound humility. To condone heresy is not an act of kindness; suspected heretics are safer in the hands of the Inquisition, which will attempt to save them, than in those of the common people who can behave with barbarous cruelty. The court must beware of being swayed by pity or anger. Merciful impulses must be tempered by respect for justice.

Cauchon, speaking next, partially discounts the dangers of licentious and easily recognised heresies. He is far more concerned with what Warwick has called Protestantism: the modern heresy of bypassing the Church and trusting in the judgement of the individual. By this the structure of the Church itself is threatened.

To Cauchon's anxieties about a popular rising on behalf of Joan, de Stogumber replies that Warwick has 800 men ready to carry out his wishes.

Joan is brought in, looking unwell. She explains that she has been made ill by eating a carp sent to her by Cauchon, and tells of the cruelties and insults inflicted on her in prison. She defends her earlier attempt to escape, and, when asked to take the oath, states that she cannot tell the whole truth, but only that part permitted by God. Members of the court demand that she be tortured, but the Bishop and Inquisitor refuse, arguing that it would achieve nothing.

Cauchon asks Joan whether she will submit herself to the Church. She replies by declaring herself unable to deny the divine source of her relevations and by refusing to obey the Church when its commands oppose those of God. She trusts in her own judgement.

Courcelles once more raises the question of the Bishop of Senlis' horse. Advising the court to disregard such trivial matters, the Promoter puts the two main charges against Joan: that she is a sorceress, and that she wears men's clothes.

Joan refuses either to accept that she has been associating with demons, or to change her clothes, arguing that, if she wore women's clothes, she would be in danger of assault from her English guards. She responds to accusations of spiritual pride by saying that she does not understand why the charge is being made. The Inquisitor replies that, in the Church's eyes, incomprehension is no defence against damnation.

Joan is then threatened with the stake, which the executioner tells her is standing ready. Suddenly recognising that her voices have misled her in telling her that she would not be burnt, Joan despairs and signs a recantation, to the fury of de Stogumber, who fears that she is about to escape. Only when Joan realises that she is to be imprisoned for life does she rebel, tearing up the recantation. She tells the court that she prefers death to perpetual banishment from the outside world. Joan is condemned as a lapsed heretic, and her excommunication is pronounced by Cauchon and the Inquisitor. Joan is taken away to the fire.

Cauchon is alarmed that the English will burn Joan at once, without going through the proper forms. The Inquisitor restrains him from interfering, telling him that a legal error may give them protection in the future. In his view, Joan did not understand the case against her, and was entirely innocent. Warwick enters as Cauchon and the Inquisitor go out to the execution. To Cauchon's complaints about the behaviour of the English soldiers, Warwick responds by expressing doubts about the validity of Cauchon's jurisdiction in Rouen, which lies outside his diocese.

Warwick stands alone in a silence which ends with the entry of the distraught de Stogumber. The actual sight of the burning of Joan has horrified him and he bitterly laments his own part in it. He tells of the soldier who gave Joan a cross of sticks. Ladvenu then describes holding up a cross before Joan, who told him to leave her and save himself from the flames. Both he and de Stogumber are convinced that Joan is with God. Warwick's only concern is that Joan's end may have a bad effect upon public opinion.

The executioner tells Warwick that Joan's body has been completely consumed, and that her heart, which would not burn, has been thrown out into the river. He believes that this is the end of the story, but Warwick closes the scene on a note of doubt.

Commentary

Scene Six of *Saint Joan*, the trial scene, is the climax of the play. When Shaw was originally drawn to the subject of Joan of Arc, the notion of dramatising her trial was one of the first things to attract him. Given his pleasure in argumentative dialogue, his outstanding success here is hardly surprising. In order to create a powerful scene, he took considerable liberties with historical fact. Seven days divided Joan's recantation from her execution but Shaw compressed those events, together with selected passages from her trial, into one long and dramatic trial scene.

Scene Six is divided into three parts. The central element, about half of the scene, presents the cross-examination of Joan by her judges on the last day of her trial. The first part, of nearly equal length, forms an introduction to Joan's entrance, telling the audience about events since Charles VII's coronation, and setting out the attitudes and conflicts which surround the trial. The brief third part covers the time of Joan's off-stage execution, reports its effect on certain characters, and, by hinting at the future, looks forward to the last scene, the Epilogue.

Like the classical Greek tragedians, Shaw was working within the limits of a well-known story. The outcome of the trial is never in doubt, and, if Joan's weakening and recantation seem to offer a brief glimpse of escape, the audience knows that this is illusory.

Shaw breaks the tension of this progress towards a violent death with moments of humour. Warwick's banter with his page, his suave politeness to the three Churchmen, may stimulate a wry smile. Even Joan, within minutes of death, can amuse us by proudly insisting that she is not a shepherd girl, and by calling Courcelles a 'noodle'. As in

Scene Four, de Stogumber provides Shaw with the means of varying the pace and the tone of the discussion. His conflicts with the moderately minded judges over whether Joan stole the Bishop's horse or danced round the fairy tree at Domrémy provoke outright laughter, while the absurd discussions over the language and clothing of a saint give Shaw an opportunity to display the comparative broadmindedness of the Inquisitor.

The Trial Scene contains one of the most famous passages in Shaw, the long Inquisitor's speech of instruction to the court. In allowing one character to talk for six or seven minutes, Shaw was, not for the first or last time, taking a considerable theatrical risk. The lucid speech sets out the case against heresy, and presents the arguments for the existence of an Inquisition. The name and role of an Inquisitor are likely to alienate any but the most rigorously Roman Catholic audience, but Shaw means us to take the speech seriously as part of his defence of Joan's judges. The Inquisitor's appeal is based upon a reasoned theory of justice, and, granted the limits within which it operates, is sensibly and intellectually argued. The critic Desmond MacCarthy speaks pertinently of the Inquisitor's 'sinister gentleness'. The careful arrangement of its propositions, and the way in which the speed builds up to its coping stone of 'justice', make it an enthralling, if challenging, piece of theatre.

The shorter and more emotional speech of Cauchon which follows, makes out a case for the maintenance of the Church. The audience is intended to respect this, even though sympathy for Joan makes it hard to accept the arguments. De Stogumber and Courcelles, determined on Joan's destruction, are opposed by Ladvenu, her only advocate. Cauchon and the Inquisitor, significantly seated above and behind these lesser characters, argue for what seems to them a greater good than mere human survival, the salvation of human souls. The Promoter, a more colourless figure than any of these, is the lawyer *par excellence* performing his task with a humourless persistence.

The early part of the cross-examination of Joan does not follow a constructive pattern. A number of issues are raised but the two important moments come later, when Cauchon asks her if she can accept the judgement of the Church, and when D'Estivet accuses her of sorcery and of wearing men's clothes. Joan's answers are, in each case, unsatisfactory to the court. She makes no attempt to defend herself, and will not express obedience to the Church.

The Inquisitor argues an abstract case in reasoned and controlled sentences, while Joan's statements are briefer and characterised by her usual pithiness of language. The report of the trial from which Shaw was working is set out in the form of a cross-examination, but Shaw is careful not to risk the monotony of simple question and answer. Joan sometimes answers a series of questions, as when D'Estivet quizzes her about her attempt to escape, but many of her remarks take the form of comments on statements made to her, or even of questions put to her judges. As the Inquisitor says at the end, Joan is often at cross-purposes with the court, unable to understand the purport of the things which are said to her. She has, however, her own straightforward truthfulness, which places her on a different, and in many ways higher, level of understanding. Immediately before she is confronted with the executioner, Joan utters two pieces of folk wisdom which show her scorn for her accusers: 'If we were as simple in the village as you are in the courts and palaces, there would soon be no wheat to make bread for you', and 'There is great wisdom in the simplicity of a beast, let me tell you; and sometimes great foolishness in the wisdom of scholars'.

Joan's longest speech in the entire play follows the destruction of her recantation. In content and style it is in complete antithesis to the recantation speech attributed to her, but actually written by Ladvenu. Where he stresses ideas of sin and repentance, Joan contrasts the limitations of her prison with the freedom of the open country. On the verge of death, she speaks with lyrical intensity of those things which she loves, and without which she would find life intolerable.

Shaw juxtaposes Joan's death off-stage with the politicking and deviousness of Warwick and the Churchmen on stage, a flatly played passage which suddenly erupts with the entry of de Stogumber, the one character in the play to truly comprehend his own shortcomings. With assistance from Ladvenu and the executioner, de Stogumber is the messenger of Greek tragedy, describing the death of the protagonist for the benefit of an audience who have not witnessed it.

2.7 EPILOGUE

Synopsis

Twenty-five years later, Charles VII is reading in bed on a windy night. In the course of the scene most of the characters of the play, living and dead, appear to him as though in a dream.

Brother Martin Ladvenu enters first, telling Charles that the sentence on Joan has been set aside at a new trial. Ladvenu leaves and Joan comes in. Charles tells her that he has been victorious in war, and that Joan herself has been rehabilitated. Joan defends the honesty of her judges, and Cauchon appears to tell her that his body has been disinterred and desecrated. Dunois confirms Charles's statement that the English have left France, and a soldier marches in singing. This is the man who gave the dying Joan a cross made of two sticks. In reward, he is released from hell for one day in the year.

De Stogumber, a half-witted old man, reiterates the lesson against cruelty which he learned at Joan's death, but he does not know her. The executioner recognises that, for all his skill, he has failed to kill the spirit of Joan. Warwick apologises profusely, regretting the unfortunate political necessity as well as the misjudgement which led to her execution.

Finally, a Vatican official of 1920 tells Joan of her canonisation. The characters, joined by the Archbishop of Rheims and the Inquisitor, each pay appropriate tribute to Joan in the form of a Te Deum, but, when she suggests that she might be resurrected, each rejects the idea and disappears.

Left alone, Joan asks God how long it will be before the earth is a fit habitation for his saints.

Commentary

The Epilogue is an essential part of *Saint Joan*. Some directors have omitted it in production, but, in doing so, they damage the whole effect of the play. Earlier writers had laid the blame for Joan's execution on her 'villainous' judges, but Shaw wants to widen the discussion, to remind the audience that the judges were guided by their own religious beliefs, convinced that they were doing their duty to Joan as well as to the Church. Shaw wants to bring home to the audience that their world, as much as hers, is unfitted for saints, and that they themselves are implicated in Joan's end. Humanity as a whole moves to destroy those of unusual ability and power. Had Shaw followed his predecessors in ending the play with the death of Joan, he could not have faced the audience with these all-important questions. Like the later German dramatist, Bertolt Brecht (1898-1956), he wanted them to go home thinking about the issues raised, not lulled into complacency by a cathartic experience. In a lighter vein, Shaw believed that no actress playing Joan would sacrifice the Epilogue: 'letting Stogumber steal the end of the play from her'.

No effort at verisimilitude is made in the Epilogue, and some aspects of the scene relate closely to developments in European drama. Shaw's decision to illustrate the Joan cult by projecting slides showing statues of her can be related to experiments with multiple forms in German expressionist drama. More importantly, the idea of Charles's dream may derive from the tradition of the 'Dream Play' inaugurated by the Swedish dramatist, August Strindberg (1849-1912). In his preface to the 'Dream Play' of 1902, Strindberg explains that in presenting the action as it takes place in the mind of the dreamer, he is able to suspend the normal strictures of realism, and to achieve a psychological rather than a literal truth.

Through his use of this device, Shaw can re-introduce figures from the earlier scenes of the play, and place them in the context of history. His motives are less psychological than schematic. In what is essentially a summing up, each character enters to outline his own role in the story of Joan, and in her posthumous reputation. The introduction of the representative of the Vatican brings the action up to 1920, but this is deliberately shown to be an anachronism when the others laugh at his clothes, just as the court ladies laughed at Joan's in Scene Two. The actual date of the action is June 1456, twenty-five years after the execution of Joan, and the time at which the rehabilitation process was completed.

The Epilogue is broken into two by the chimes of the clock, another insistent reminder of the passage of time. The descent into hell of the soldier at the end of the play may even be a comic parody of the end of Christopher Marlowe's *Doctor Faustus*, where Faustus is dragged off to his fate, or, more probably with the opera-loving Shaw, of the close of Mozart's *Don Giovanni*, where the hero is dispatched by the statue of an outraged father.

Shaw's dreamer, Charles VII, reacts to each of the visitors in his usual way. He is a man without ideals or pretensions, but with enough wry common sense to bring out the essential issues. Charles's speech patterns are colloquial and practical, contrasting markedly with those of other characters who, engaged in putting a case, speak in a manner appropriate to their argument. Cauchon uses his usual ecclesiastical rhetoric, the Vatican official a pompous twentieth-century jargon. In Charles's conversations with Joan, however, there is a sense that a genuine dialogue is being carried on, and that these two characters are indeed able to communicate, and to talk naturally.

Brother Martin Ladvenu puts Shaw's own case about the comparative fairness of the original trial and the dishonesty of the later revisions.

Ladvenu's way of piling up sentences and clauses to reach an oratorical climax, matches his striking use of Biblical imagery: 'the white robe of innocence is cleansed from the smirch of the burning faggots'. Ladvenu's voice is that of those who will sanctify Joan, yet Charles rightly points out that she was not 'that sort', as Joan herself proves on arrival. Her character is unchanged. Her questions are practical ones about the conduct of the war, and she retains that curious mixture of humility and pride on which the Inquisitor commented in the trial scene.

As a commentary on the lasting effects of Joan's career, the Epilogue is fairly encouraging. France has been saved, the King has become Charles the Victorious. De Stogumber has been purged of his cruelty. The possibility that Joan has achieved more by her death than her life is suggested by parallels with Christ. Ladvenu, like the Christmas angels, tells Charles that he brings 'glad tidings of great joy'. His final lines 'God forbid that I should have no share in her, nor she in me!' echo the Anglican communion service: 'we may evermore dwell in him, and he in us'. Joan's brief appearance resembles that of the resurrected Christ after the harrowing of hell, but, like Christ, she is too disturbing to remain upon earth for very long. Joan has no comment on the after-life, but the soldier tells us that hell is an interesting and human place. His one day off was like 'a wet Sunday', until he got used to it. As in the earlier *Man and Superman*, Shaw implies by this that most people would find heaven very dull. Joan is one of those who may enjoy heaven. She tells the King that 'my head was in the skies; and the glory of God was upon me; and, man or woman, I should have bothered you as long as your noses were in the mud'. The idea that men and women seek out their own proper setting is echoed in Charles's complacent remark that he keeps his nose 'pretty close to the ground'. Earth is not fit for saints, and those who have lived contentedly on earth will find hell a natural extension of their earthly life.

The desertion of Joan at the end of the Epilogue parallels that in Scene Five, while the anticlimax which follows the revised Te Deum performs a similar dramatic function to Joan's recantation in Scene Six. All three scenes leave Joan in isolation.

2.8 THE PREFACE

Shaw's Preface to *Saint Joan*, completed in May 1924, was intended to accompany the published text. It was Shaw's usual practice to write his prefaces after the plays; as a result, some of them have little to do with the play to which they belong. Writing and performance of *Heartbreak House* were extended over a long period, and by the time that Shaw came to write the preface, his mind was already engaged with other issues. By contrast, the preface to *Saint Joan* is centrally concerned with the themes of the drama, perhaps because play writing, performance and preface were all accomplished within about a year.

Shaw analysed the function of this particular preface in the section entitled 'Modern Distortions of Joan's History':

> The romance of her [Joan's] rise, the tragedy of her execution, and the comedy of the attempts of posterity to make amends for that execution, belong to my play and not to my preface, which must be confined to a sober essay on the facts.

The author explains that his aim in this 'sober essay' is to correct the standard works of reference which 'all break down on the melodramatic legend of the wicked bishop and the entrapped maiden and the rest of it'. Later he declares that there are no villains in his play. If he has been too kind to Joan's accusers, it is part of his attempt to make them intelligible. Their eloquence is a way of expressing what they would have said had they understood their own position.

The reader of the Preface may feel that he or she has already heard all the arguments in the course of the play, but, studied carefully, it adds a good deal to our understanding of *Saint Joan*.

Shaw begins with a sweeping attempt to place Joan, stating that she was a Protestant, a nationalist and a rational dresser. He compares her to the Greek philosopher Socrates (468–400/399 BC), another clear-sighted genius who inadvertently made others feel stupid. Not surprisingly, both were executed. Socrates's accuser, 'if born 2300 years later, might have been picked out of any first class carriage on a suburban railway during the evening or morning rush from or to the City'.

This sentence exemplifies the main thrust and intention of the Preface, which continually returns to an assertion that, for all our feelings of superiority, modern man is no better morally than fifteenth-century man. We credit ourselves with more tolerance, but Shaw insists that tolerance is relative to the strains placed upon a particular society at a particular time. Tolerance operates in different ways in different conditions. Joan's trial is comparable with those of the English nurse

Edith Cavell (shot as a spy by the German army in the First World War), or of Roger Casement (hanged by the English as a traitor for his part in the Irish rebellion). Shaw makes the same point through Warwick's definition of a traitor in Scene Four of *Saint Joan*: 'one not wholly devoted to our English interests'. In England, the Preface tells us, outsiders like the suffragette leader, Emmeline Pankhurst (1858–1928), or parents who choose not to send their children to school are treated with the same lack of tolerance as Joan. In Shaw's view, a world unable to tolerate such originality will be exploded by evolutionary forces.

As a Protestant, Shaw cannot believe in Joan's voices, but he is not prepared to dismiss her as a crank or a liar. Instead, he puts forward a case for her inspiration and vision, and for her greatness as a proponent of the evolutionary appetite. He declares that in the 'anti-metaphysical' modern world, men and women are just as credulous as Joan's contemporaries. Following a favourite Shavian argument, he insists that modern belief in doctors is as absurd as any medieval superstition. Medieval belief in an afterlife represented a useful check on human greed and ruthlessness. If a medieval man said the earth was flat, he was stating a self-evident truth, a point which La Trémouille makes bluntly in Scene Two of *Saint Joan*. If we now believe that the world is round, Shaw says, most of us are in no position to prove it.

Shaw takes up the argument, inherent in the play, that the real Joan cannot have been at all like the romantic nineteenth-century image of her. He criticises two of her biographers, Mark Twain (1835–1910) and Andrew Lang (1844–1912), for not trying to understand the Middle Ages, and for condemning the Church and Cauchon out of hand. Shakespeare, with no historical sources at all, was even further adrift. From the records Shaw concludes that Joan was not a beauty, nor, as the daughter of a leading man of the village, was she a poverty-stricken shepherd girl. Her choice of masculine dress was not a sign of divine inspiration, but an indication of her choice to live like a soldier and to go to war. Shaw comments that the convention that women should stay at home while men fight results from the need to reproduce mankind, not from any inherent quality in the sexes. Joan, he insists, knew about artillery and was able, like Napoleon, to judge the military situation. She was a 'born boss' and her prudish reforms in the French army, stopping swearing and banning camp-followers, served to increase its efficiency.

Shaw is putting forward arguments which do not undermine Joan's greatness, but which place her in a secular rather than a religious context. These ideas are all touched upon in the dialogue of the play, but, in the Preface, Shaw states them more directly and more positively. He explains Joan's failure by her youthful inexperience and her lack of subtlety. Her refusal to obey orders, and her reiterated references back to God aroused irritation and scepticism, leaving her undefended. Uneducated, she did not have the intellectual power to understand the workings of Church and state which destroyed her.

Towards the end of the Preface, Shaw addresses himself to the question of the Catholic Church. He argues that all human beings prefer the company of the mediocre to that of the exceptional. As a result, the saints are unlikely to be represented in the Church hierarchy. Joan's accusers mistook the Church Militant, to which they belonged, for the Church Triumphant, assuming that their fallible opinions represented the will of God. The Church needs to be responsive to change, and can only survive through fruitful interaction with free-thinkers and reformers.

Shaw's final blast in the Preface is a more personal one, directed against those critics and fashionable audiences who argued for the omission of the Epilogue and for a shorter play. As a dramatist, Shaw says that he favours those audiences, often found in provincial cities, who like *Saint Joan* as it is, a three and a half-hour play, with one interval.

3 THEMES AND ISSUES

3.1 JOAN OR ARC: THE HISTORICAL FIGURE

Joan of Arc was born in about 1412 or 1413 in the village of Domrémy on the borders of Lorraine and Champagne in what is now North-Eastern France. During her childhood, the country around her home was repeatedly ravaged by rival armies during the later stages of the Hundred Years War between England and France. The war had begun in 1337 when Edward III of England laid claim to the French crown through his mother, Isabella of France, but it had its origins in territorial disputes stretching back over two centuries. Events tended to favour the English who won two great victories: Crécy, under Edward III in 1346, and Agincourt, under Henry V in 1415. After Agincourt the Burgundians formed an alliance with the English, and in 1428 their united army, which already controlled large areas of Northern France, laid siege to Orleans as a first step to the conquest of the South.

Early in 1429, Joan left her home in Domrémy, believing that voices from God had instructed her to raise the siege of Orléans, and to crown the Dauphin as Charles VII of France in Rheims Cathedral. Without the traditional coronation, Charles's status was uncertain; in 1422 the infant Henry VI of England, son of the victor of Agincourt, had also been proclaimed King of France. Joan persuaded the Dauphin to let her fight with his army, and she was present when Orléans was relieved in May 1429. Rheims was behind the enemy lines but after a series of French victories, at Jargeau, Meung, Beaugency and Patay, the coronation took place there in July. Joan's assault on Paris in September failed, and in May 1439 she was captured by the Burgundians at

Compiègne and subsequently sold to the English. Her long trial at Rouen began in February 1431 and ended with her execution by burning on 30 May. Pierre Cauchon, Bishop of Beauvais (d.1442) and Richard de Beauchamp, Earl of Warwick (1382-1439), were both deeply implicated in the processes which led to Joan's death.

The war continued until 1453, but the relief of Orléans marked the turning of the tide against the English. Charles VII regained Paris in 1437, and in 1450 and 1452 two inquiries into Joan's sentence were instituted. After a long investigation in 1455-6 the sentence was reversed. Joan was canonised by the Roman Catholic Church in 1920.

3.2 SHAW'S SOURCES

Shaw visited Orléans for the first time in September 1913. In a letter written from there he told the actress, Mrs Patrick Campbell, of a projected Joan of Arc play which would begin immediately after Joan's martyrdom 'with the sweeping up of the cinders and orange peel'. The next scene would present Joan's arrival in heaven. Just as God is about to damn the English, Joan produces the remaining fragment of the simple crucifix made for her by an English soldier, and says: 'you cannot damn the common people of England, represented by that soldier because a poor cowardly riff raff of barons and bishops were too futile to resist the devil'. Shaw glosses Joan's words with 'That soldier is the only redeeming figure in the whole business'.

This statement of intent is important, not simply because it underlines Shaw's interest in the subject of Joan, but also because of its emphasis on the aftermath of her story. It implies that the Epilogue came into Shaw's imagination first rather than last. Shaw's chief concern is with the question of personal and national responsibility. That remained central to the play as he wrote it, though the barons and bishops were scarcely 'poor riff raff', and the soldier's role was reduced to a brief appearance in the Epilogue.

Shaw's major historical source for *Saint Joan* was Jules Quicherat's transcription of the official records of Joan's trial and of the rehabilitation processes. Shaw cheerfully acknowledged his dependence upon T. Douglas Murray's 1902 translation of Quicherat's work, and told several people, including the first English actress to play Joan, Sybil Thorndike: 'This is the easiest play I've ever written. All the words were there for me'. The dramatist was exaggerating, but he did draw extensively upon the records, particularly for the trial scene, where he took some of Joan's lines directly from Murray's translation. The examples which follow are representative:

Shaw:

JOAN. I will do a lady's work in the house – spinning or weaving – against any woman in Rouen.

Murray:

JOAN. Yes, I learnt to spin and sew; in sewing and spinning I fear no woman in Rouen.

Shaw:

JOAN. If I am not [in a state of grace] , may God bring me to it: if I am, may God keep me in it!

Murray:

JOAN. If I am not, may God place me there; if I am, may God keep me so.

Shaw:

COURCELLES. Does he not appear to you as a naked man?
JOAN. Do you think God cannot afford clothes for him?

Murray:

QUESTION. Was he naked?
JOAN. Do you think God has not wherewithal to clothe him?

Joan's statements on her right to try to escape, her refusal to reveal the whole truth, her account of her own background; all of these are closely modelled on the account in the trial records. Murray validates Shaw's decision to make Joan a rough and practical country girl, not an ideal figure of romance. Shaw was not writing a documentary, however, and it should be recognised that he isolated from the long transcription only those statements which furthered his own argument. He then rearranged them so as to lay stress on particular issues, and to increase their dramatic punch.

This is evident during the excommunication of Joan, where Shaw selects the most striking and vivid lines from Murray's four pages of sentence and excommunication, and then divides them between Cauchon and the Inquisitor.

Shaw:

> CAUCHON. We decree that thou art a relapsed heretic.
>
> THE INQUISITOR. Cast out from the unity of the Church.
>
> CAUCHON. Sundered from her body.
>
> THE INQUISITOR. Infected with the leprosy of heresy.
>
> CAUCHON. A member of Satan.
>
> THE INQUISITOR. We declare that thou must be excommunicate.
>
> CAUCHON. And now we do cast thee out, segregate thee, and abandon thee to secular power.
>
> THE INQUISITOR. Admonishing the same secular power that it moderate its judgment of thee in respect of death and division of limbs. [*He resumes his seat*].
>
> CAUCHON. And if any true sign of penitence appear in thee, to permit our Brother Martin to administer to thee the sacrament of penance.

Murray:

We declare that thou must be abandoned and that We do abandon thee to the secular authority, as a member of Satan, separate from the Church, infected with the leprosy of heresy, in order that thou mayst not corrupt also the other members of Christ; praying this same power, that, as concerns death and the mutilation of the limbs, it may be pleased to moderate its judgement; and if true signs of penitence should appear in thee, that the Sacrament of Penance may be administered to thee.

3.3 SHAW'S NINETEENTH-CENTURY PREDECESSORS

Shaw was right to find the record of the trial a remarkable document, and an effective antidote to nineteenth-century accounts of Joan. He told friends that Murray's work was the only historical book which he had consulted, but he was aware of various biographies and historical dramas, to some of which he refers in the Preface. Shaw's general view of them is summed up in his instructions to Sybil Thorndike: 'Forget them, I'll tell you what to think'.

Shaw had probably seen *Jeanne D'arc (Called the Maid)*, a play of 1871 by the Victorian dramatist, Tom Taylor, in Dublin. In some respects Shaw's choice of scenes for his play closely resembles Taylor's.

Both open at Vaucouleurs, and follow with scenes at Chinon, Orléans, Rheims and Rouen. Shaw's play is, however, very different in effect, not only because of his invention of a scene between Cauchon and Warwick (Scene Four) and of an Epilogue, but also because he deliberately avoids theatrical cliché by not presenting Joan's most triumphant moments. With the sole exception of the end of Scene Two, all opportunities for spectacular events are avoided. Shaw's Scene Three ends before the raising of the siege of Orléans, his Scene Five starts after the coronation at Rheims, Joan is burned off stage in Scene Six. Shaw's attempt to defend Joan's judges, and his analysis of the underlying social context of the play, are again entirely uncharacteristic of nineteenth-century historical and costume drama.

A more famous theatrical version of the life of Joan of Arc was *Die Jungfrau von Orleans* of 1801 by the German romantic writer, Friedrich Schiller (1759–1805). In Schiller's play, Joan is protected by God only as long as she resists human love. Her passion for an English soldier, Lionel, leads directly to a fatal injury on the battlefield. Numerous plays and operas were based upon Schiller's version, which Shaw characterises as 'romantic nonsense' and 'beglamoured sentimentality' in the Preface to *Saint Joan*.

Shaw also refers to the biographies of Joan written by Mark Twain and Andrew Lang. Lang was writing in reaction to the 1908 life of Joan by a Frenchman, Anatole France (1844–1024), who interpreted Joan as a puppet of the clergy. Shaw takes Twain and Lang to task for misinterpreting the Middle Ages, and for allowing anti-Catholic prejudice to run away with them. According to Shaw, Lang, a Scot, and Twain, an American, both believed that 'Catholic bishops who burnt heretics were persecutors capable of any villainy; that all heretics were Albigensians or Husites [sic] or Jews or Protestants of the highest character; and that the Inquisition was a Chamber of Horrors invented expressly and exclusively for such burnings'. (Both the Albigensians and the Hussites were late medieval groups who found themselves in opposition to the Catholic church, the Albigensians in southern France, the Hussites in what is now Czechoslovakia.)

Shaw himself seeks to avoid distortion by setting Joan firmly into her historical context, by avoiding prejudice, and by interpreting the characters in her story through a sound understanding of human nature. His strongest challenge to the nineteenth-century presentation of Joan comes in his contention that her trial was not a travesty of justice, as Lang and Twain had asserted, but careful and conscientious by the standards of the contemporary legal system. Shaw clearly states this in the Epilogue and the Preface, as well as in the Programme Note which he wrote for the first production. He condemns the posthumous treatment of her judges: 'For these slanders of the Church and the Inquisition there is not a shred of evidence in the records of the trial. Joan's judges were as straightforward as Joan herself; and the law took its regular course.'

Shaw was aware that he had bent over backwards in his reinterpretation of Cauchon and the Inquisition. In the Preface he admits that he has flattered 'Cauchon nearly as much as the melodramatist vilifies him'. Historians accuse Shaw in his turn of being no more accurate than Lang or Twain, and of misreading his sources. Cauchon's refusal to torture Joan, which Shaw sees as a result of sensitivity and intelligence, is more accurately explained as part of a deliberate attempt to appear to be acting legally. In the eyes of most historians, the judges were all determined upon Joan's execution, and the result of the trial was never in doubt. If Shaw's characterisation of Cauchon is too kindly, however, there is general agreement that Joan's treatment was what might be expected in a medieval court, and the verdict was entirely consistent with the legal processes of the time.

3.4 SHAW AND HISTORY

Shaw's intention to present the real Joan in his play, together with the use of contemporary documents, might suggest that he was attempting a historical reconstruction. In his own terms, he no doubt felt that he was. He later went so far as to congratulate himself on his accuracy in the Preface to his later historical play, *In Good King Charles's Golden Days* (1939): 'my own chief history plays, Caesar and Cleopatra and St Joan, are fully documented chronicle plays of this type. Familiarity with them should get a student safely through examination papers on their periods'. *Good King Charles*, although subtitled 'A History Lesson', is very far from being historically accurate, and Shaw's comments are perhaps more closely related to his prejudice against exam papers than to his treatment of his sources.

The Preface and the Programme Note written for *Saint Joan* in any case declare that the presentation of exact historical truth upon the stage is impossible. Shaw explains that he has compressed events which took days or weeks into single scenes. Most of the characters are based upon real originals. The soldier in the Epilogue is given credence by persistent legend, and even the fictional de Stogumber is based upon the unnamed chaplain who accused Cauchon of trying to save Joan: 'I have given him a Somerset name which is appropriate when mispronounced', writes Shaw, Stogumber being the name of a Somerset village. Shaw admits that Jean Dunois (c.1403-68), the natural son of Louis d'Orléans, brother of Charles VI, has been conflated with another French nobleman, Jean Duc d'Alençon (1409-76), and justifies this by saying that the two men must have been very much alike. The dramatist naughtily points out that this conflation has saved theatre managements a salary.

Like the Italian historian, Benedetto Croce (1866-1952), Shaw believed that history must be read through the perspective of one's own age. *Saint Joan* tells us something about Shaw's attitude to contemporary issues and events. He was writing soon after the end of another long and hard campaign on French soil, the 1914-18 war. During the war, Shaw had vehemently protested against the same war-mongering and jingoism which characterise de Stogumber's attitude to Joan. Even more topical was the republican struggle in Ireland, which ended with the establishment of the Free State in 1921. In the Preface, Shaw compares Joan's trial to two contemporary ones, those of Edith Cavell (an English nurse shot by the Germans as a spy in 1915) and of Roger Casement (an Irishman executed for treason against England in 1916). The republican cause presented Shaw with a very close parallel to Joan's determination to liberate France from a foreign yoke. Some of Joan's remarks about Englishmen who try to subdue and govern other races could have an application to the then still extant British Empire.

Shaw's conflation of past and present is accentuated by the characters' language and thought processes. From the start audiences were disturbed by the curious amalgam of Joan's rustic expressions ('art' for are not; 'wilt' for will you; 'goddam' for Englishman) and the contrastingly modern anachronisms which sometimes turn up in the same speeches ('staff officer', 'military dugouts', 'gosh', 'spunk'). Dunois' explanation of Joan's unpopularity in Scene Five: 'Do ambitious politicians love the climbers who take the front seats from them?' is a clear reference to the modern House of Commons. In the same vein, the Archbishop of Rheims says of the Dauphin: 'He never has a suit of clothes that I would throw to a curate'. Shaw's intention in this is anti-romantic. He denies the existence of an inherent cultural difference between one age and another, and avoids the escapism associated with Victorian historical drama. He told Sybil Thorndike, after the first London performance of the play, that the elaborate costumes and sets had spoiled the effect, that he preferred the casual clothes worn in the rehearsal.

Shaw's approach here separates him from the romantic historical tradition often associated with the Scottish novelist Sir Walter Scott (1771-1832). Scott's novels represent the greatest single influence upon nineteenth-century historical literature, and he did much to promulgate a legend of the middle ages as an era of colourful pageantry. Shaw dismisses Scott in the Preface to *Saint Joan* as a writer who 'enjoyed medieval history as a string of Border romances rather than as a record of a high European civilization based on a catholic faith'. Another characteristic of Scott's writing, however, brings him far closer to Shaw, and recommended him to the Marxist critic of the historical novel, Georg Lukács (1885-1971). As Lukács noted, many of Scott's novels take place in periods of change and of historical evolution, when one culture comes into conflict with another. In presenting Joan as a precursor of a new, post-medieval age, as well as in his concern for her as a strong individual, crushed by the self-interest of large forces, Shaw was following a traditional pattern.

3.5 JOAN AS A REVOLUTIONARY HEROINE

Shaw is at pains to present Joan to the audience as a revolutionary figure. In the fourth, fifth and sixth scenes of the play, the two rival forces of Church and state unite in opposition to Joan, whose independence of mind, common sense and vision are anathema to both. These themes are expressed with exceptional clarity and dynamism in Scene Four, where Shaw epitomises Warwick and Cauchon through the two terms which they employ in attempting to explain their own motives for fearing Joan's influence. Both words, 'protestantism' and 'nationalism', are introduced as though they are new to the speakers, and as though they are in course of evolution from their original roots (in the verb, to protest and the noun, nation). In one recent production they were not pronounced in current fashion, but in a way which stressed their derivation, and reminded the audience of their original sources (nation-alism and protest-antism).

Shaw's Joan is seen as a forerunner of two changes which marked the end of the Middle Ages. The first was the Protestant challenge to

the Catholic Church which resulted in the religious and political movement known as the Reformation. Its effect was to end the power of
the Papacy in parts of central and northern Europe. The second was
the sense of allegiance to a nation, and to the monarch as representative of that nation, which Warwick sees as threatening the allegiance
of men and women to their feudal overlords. In addressing herself to
the Dauphin, admittedly through the intermediary of her overlord,
Robert de Baudricourt, Joan is guided by a vision of France united
under a strong monarch.

In the same way, Joan addresses herself directly to God, through
the medium of saints, and so side-steps the Catholic Church, which
has always believed that man can only approach God through the
Church Militant. As Shaw points out in both play and Preface, the
Church was already under attack. The cleric, John Wyclif (c.1329-84)
translated much of the Bible into English, and was several times charged
with propagating heretical opinions, among them a belief that all
authority, secular and ecclesiastical derived from God. Shaw's Cauchon
insists that all Englishmen are heretical at heart, and complains that
Wyclif was allowed to die in his bed instead of facing execution. In
the same passage, Cauchon refers to John Hus (c.1369-1415), a
Bohemian reformer, who was influenced by the writings of Wyclif.
Lured to the Council of Constance with a safe-conduct from the
Emperor, Hus was condemned and burnt. His followers continued his
struggle in the Hussite wars, and Joan herself is said to have challenged
the Hussites to return to the Church in a letter written in 1430, the
year of her death.

Shaw believed that Joan had much in common with Wyclif and
Hus, whose 'heresy' was similar to hers. Cauchon, who shares the
belief, sees them all as agents of the devil, bent upon damning men
by destroying the power of the Church. When the Inquisitor refers
to other heretical movements which advocated polygamy and sexual
excess, he is evidently (and anachronistically) thinking of another
figure who fascinated Shaw, John of Leyden, founder of the so-called
Kingdom of God at Munster, in Germany. John of Leyden was brutally
executed there in 1536. Shaw discusses him in the Preface to *Androcles
and the Lion* (1915), and sees him as one of the few people to have
attempted to live according to Christ's commands. In Shaw's eyes the
attempt was 'grotesque' and the people 'inadequate'. Cauchon too
insists that the danger to the Church comes, not from such extremists,
but from emergent 'protestants', like Joan.

Shaw had the benefit of hindsight. Martin Luther, born in 1483, fifty-two years after Joan's death, was to fulfil Cauchon's prophecies about the undermining of the Church's authority. On the English political front, the later Yorkist monarchs and the Tudor Kings progressively concentrated power into their own hands. Warwick's famous son-in-law Warwick the 'kingmaker' (1428–71), was to be one of the victims of the changes which Warwick dreads. Historians even suggest that Shaw was already behind the times in this prophecy, as he was too far ahead of it in turning Joan into a Protestant.

3.6 THE WANING OF THE MIDDLE AGES

Shaw underlines his general statement that this was a time of change, with a number of smaller details. He knew that one of the most serious challenges to the Church's teaching came from those scientists, of whom Galileo Galilei (1564–1642) is the most famous, who taught that the earth is round, not flat. Shaw slips the issue into the conversation between the Archbishop and La Trémouille in Scene Two, where the Archbishop speaks of 'a new spirit rising in men: we are at the dawning of a wider epoch. If I were a simple monk, and had not to rule men, I should seek peace for my spirit with Aristotle and Pythagoras rather than with the saints and their miracles.' When La Trémouille asks about the identity of Pythagoras, the Archbishop replies: 'A sage who held that the earth is round, and that it moves around the sun', to which La Trémouille replies: 'What an utter fool! Couldn't he use his eyes?' The reference to astronomy here is reinforced by the classical context. The Renaissance, which signalled the end of the Middle Ages, was fuelled by the rediscovery of Greek and Roman literature and art.

La Trémouille's ignorance of Pythagoras may have something to do with the fact he cannot read. The spread of literacy naturally attracted Shaw's attention as part of a changing pattern of behaviour. It is the subject of a number of pointed passages in the play. La Trémouille, according to Shaw's stage direction, is not ashamed of his illiteracy, and tells the Dauphin contemptuously that 'reading is about all you are fit for'. In the Epilogue, Charles is found 'reading in bed, or rather looking at the pictures in Fouquet's Boccaccio'. Joan, who cannot read either, is as critical as La Trémouille: 'Fallen asleep over thy silly book' she tells the King. Warwick, like Charles, prefers looking at the pictures, rather than studying the text. His Book of Hours is a hand-copied illuminated manuscript, one of the finest productions of the Middle Ages. Here too, change is imminent. Even in 1429 Warwick tells de Stogumber that 'nowadays, instead of looking at books, people read them. A book might as well be one of those orders for bacon and bran that you are scribbling'. Again Shaw had the benefit of superior knowledge. By 1448, nineteen years later, Johann Gutenberg (c.1399-1468) had already begun to make moveable type. Shaw's sympathy was probably with Warwick. As a friend of the Victorian designer and printer William Morris (1834-96), he understood that modern printing techniques had destroyed much of the beauty of a book page. His own books were printed in a plain old Caslon type, with off centre title pages, and he even insisted that apostrophes were omitted, so that his own work should not be covered with irritating little dots. Shaw's spelling is characteristically idiosyncratic. In some ways his usage is consciously archaic, as in 'Shakespear' and 'shewing', although it could be said that his choice of 'o' instead of the more usual 'ou' in 'savior' or 'laborer' also approximates to modern American practice.

3.7 JOAN AS A BOURGEOISE

Protestantism first took root in those countries where a strong entrepreneurial class existed. In making Joan into a Protestant heroine, Shaw associated her with the growth of a capitalist class in France. In Scene One, de Baudricourt tells de Poulengey that Joan is not a peasant girl, but a bourgeoise. De Baudricourt's use of the word is anachronistic, and historians insist that Shaw is using a term applicable only to later periods of history. Anxious to counter the romantic view that Joan had come from a poor and humble background, Shaw firmly establishes her family origins through de Baudricourt:

I know her class exactly. Her father came here last year to represent his village in a lawsuit: he is one of their notables. A farmer. Not a gentleman farmer: he makes money by it, and lives by it. Still, not a laborer. Not a mechanic. He might have a cousin a lawyer, or in the Church. People of this sort may be of no account socially; but they can give a lot of bother to the authorities.

Shaw's Joan resents suggestions that she had been a shepherdess. She may (like the real Joan) occasionally have helped in the fields, but she insists that her usual place was in the house, helping her mother with the weaving and sewing. To Shaw, the issue was an important one. He insisted that Joan, like Christ, was not one of the labouring poor. Had she been a true peasant, her mission could not have been undertaken.

A member of the middle class, Shaw's heroine is scornful of aristocratic modes of warfare. Arguing with Dunois in Scene Five, Joan tells him that the days of knights in armour are over, and fighting for ransom money with them. War has become a serious business. Shaw believed that Joan was a pioneer in the employment of artillery. In Scene Three, she tells Dunois to use the 'big guns . . . you cannot fight stone walls with horses; you must have guns, and much bigger guns too'. Here Joan is the voice of the new age, Dunois that of the conservative: 'Half the time the artillery is more trouble than it is worth.' Dunois' point is a good one historically. At this date, guns were primitive, forged rather than cast, and they inflicted relatively little damage.

3.8 JOAN AS A FEMINIST

The heroine's assertion of the right to think for herself, cuts across not only feudal and religious conventions, but sexual mores as well. Joan's contemporaries were preoccupied with her virginity, which even her enemies found themselves unable seriously to dispute. Her role as a 'maid' or 'la Pucelle', an important part of her image while she was alive, was central to the posthumous cult. Neither in the Preface nor in the play does Shaw show much interest in this aspect of the Joan legend. Instead, he prefers to state that Joan, while not unattractive, has no sex appeal, and is exempt from enfeebling sexual preoccupations. In Scene One, de Poulengey angrily responds to de Baudicourt's 'hands off her' with a statement that Joan's purity is sacrosanct. He asserts, in an echo of a remark made in the trial records, that the soldiers in the guardroom have not said 'a word that has anything to do with her being a woman'. For Shaw Joan was not the appealing woman depicted by nineteenth-century artists:

> All the men who alluded to the matter declared emphatically that she was unattractive sexually to a degree that seemed to them miraculous, considering that she was in the bloom of youth, and neither ugly, awkward, deformed, nor unpleasant in her person.

Shaw's Joan is a 'pioneer of rational dressing for women', a cause to which he was himself devoted. Her adoption of male dress is a factor of great importance at her trial; her accusors, like those in the historical trial, return to it again and again. For the historical Joan, what she wore reflected the nature of her mission from God. Only after her trial did she declare a practical reason for wearing male dress in prison, a fear of assault by her English guards. Shaw accepts this line of reasoning, but, like Joan herself, regards it as a secondary one. Joan wears male dress because she wants to fight, and Shaw gives his heroine some revealing lines on the subject. She tells Dunois: 'I am a soldier: I do not want to be thought of as a woman. I will not dress as a woman. I do not care for the things that women care for.' Following her recantation she contemplates with distaste a return to Domrémy: 'I could drag about in a skirt, I could let the banners and the trumpets and the knights and soldiers pass me and leave me behind with the other women.' The only 'other women' in Shaw's play are the stereotyped court ladies who surround the Duchess de la Trémouille in Scene Two.

T. S. Eliot, writing in 1924, responded sharply to these aspects of Shaw's Joan, calling her 'a great middle-class reformer . . . her place is a little higher than Mrs Pankhurst'. Shaw would probably have accepted the judgement. Women are usually the stronger characters in his post-war plays, and he himself describes Joan as an 'insufferable', 'strong-minded scheming woman', as someone who 'bullied everyone'.

3.9 JOAN AND CREATIVE EVOLUTION

Like the Victorian thinker and historian, Thomas Carlyle (1795–1881), Shaw believed that mankind could only move forward if great men and women emerged to lead it. Democracy spelt mediocrity, greed and incompetence. Shaw described this evolutionary power as the Life Force.

The historical plays which precede *Saint Joan* are dominated by Shaw's discussion of the nature of genius. The first of them, the short piece, *The Man of Destiny* (1896), presents an imaginary incident during Napoleon's Italian campaign. With his hard-headed realism and power of decision, Napoleon refuses to be overwhelmed by sexual impulse. He is a recognisable Shavian hero, defined, like Joan in the opening scenes of *Saint Joan*, through a series of striking contrasts with those weaker than himself.

Shaw's Julius Caesar in *Caesar and Cleopatra* (1898) is more like-able than his Napoleon, but he has many of the same characteristics. Caesar's will is supreme, and the contrast to the passionate excesses of Shakespeare's *Antony and Cleopatra* is insisted upon in the Preface (1912): 'Are ye impatient with me? Do ye crave for a story of an unchaste woman? Hath the name of Cleopatra tempted ye hither? Ye foolish ones.' Shaw's Caesar reveals his greatness through a capacity to show mercy, and through his awareness that patterns of violence and revenge are self-perpetuating. On the other hand we are made aware that this enlightened philosophy is self-interested; clemency is a useful adjunct of temporal power. Following a stage further, Caesar can be seen to have certain attributes associated with Christ, as have Barbara Undershaft in *Major Barbara* and Joan herself. Though her powers are limited, Joan shares with Napoleon and Caesar the attri-bute of military prowess, a sign, in Shaw's view, of a great mind. In *The Man of Destiny* he dwells with delight on Napoleon's experiments with cannon, a foretaste of Joan's interest in artillery. Comparing Joan to Napoleon in the Preface to *Saint Joan*, Shaw comments that Joan was innocent, benevolent, frank and modest, while Napoleon, a 'mental giant' of 'terrifying ability', was none of these things. Even so he feels able to speak of them in the same breath. Shaw's Joan is a person of magnetism, cut off by death from fulfilling her potential.

In Scene Four, Cauchon speaks of the 'Will to Power in the world', the will which stimulates great battles of Church and state. He is quoting from Friedrich Nietzche, the German philosopher (1844-1900), who argued that the strenuous exercise of the will is a means of seizing power and of bringing about a change in the world. Joan's achievement is to create a nation by strenuously uniting the country in face of the enemy, and overcoming the spirit of defeatism. She is a fighting saint and represents a concept which increasingly excited Shaw in his later years. Shaw, himself a vegetarian and teetotaller, makes much of her moderate and simple diet, which, he implies, allows her to make ef-fective use of her personal gifts. Her army reforms result from a combination of simple common sense and fierce personal Puritanism.

3.10 SHAW AND JOAN'S 'VOICES'

In the Preface to the play Shaw sums up his feelings about Joan's mystical experience: 'it happens that, my fashion being Victorian and my family habit Protestant, I find myself unable to attach any such objective validity to the form of Joan's visions'. He interpreted Joan's voices as the expressions of her inner convictions, clothed by a pious country girl in the form of three saints, Catherine, Margaret and Michael. Joan's visions result from the force of creative evolution of which she is an agent.

In Scene Five, Joan tells Dunois that she hears her voices in the sound of the church bells. Shaw seems to be suggesting that his heroine is innocently practising self-hypnosis, but it is important to recognise that he was again drawing upon Joan's own words. The dialogue between de Baudricourt and Joan in Scene One also suggests a rational, rather than mystical explanation:

ROBERT. How do you mean? voices?

JOAN. I hear voices telling me what to do. They come from God.

ROBERT. They come from your imagination.

JOAN. Of course. That is how the messages of God come to us.

Shaw is careful to establish that, whatever its origin, the advice which Joan attributes to the voices is sound, even inspired. The relief of Orléans and the coronation of Charles VII are political necessities if France is to survive. Joan's greatness lies in persuading others that these seemingly impossible tasks lie within their grasp. A streak of opportunism runs through the play, as the need for a leader of Joan's calibre is measured against desperate circumstances. Poulengey tells de Baudricourt: 'I think the girl herself is a bit of a miracle. Anyhow, she is the last card left in our hand. Better play her than throw up the game.' La Hire adopts a similar point of view when he argues with the Archbishop: 'if he [de Baudricourt] thinks she can beat the English, all the rest of the army will think so too'.

A similar pragmatism lies behind Shaw's approach to one of the most popular tales in the Joan legend, her correct identification of the Dauphin on her arrival at court. The Archbishop explains this in advance to La Trémouille, telling him that Joan will have no difficulty in distinguishing the Dauphin since 'everybody in Chinon knows . . . that the Dauphin is the meanest-looking and worst-dressed figure in the Court, and that the man with the blue beard is Gilles de Rais'. When La Trémouille responds by saying that this would not be a miracle, the Archbishop tells him:

THE ARCHBISHOP. A miracle, my friend, is an event which creates faith. That is the purpose and nature of miracles. They may seem very wonderful to the people who witness them, and very simple to those who perform them. That does not matter; if they confirm or create faith they are miracles.

LA TRÉMOUILLE. Even when they are frauds, do you mean?

THE ARCHBISHOP. Frauds deceive. An event which creates faith does not deceive; therefore it is not a fraud, but a miracle.

Joan's recognition of the Dauphin is one of her three 'miracles' in Shaw's play. The other two, the hens' resumption of egg-laying, and the change of wind at Orléans are clearly explicable in terms of the law of probabilities. As Cauchon says, these miracles are not impressive and Joan herself does not claim that they are. Shaw is not attempting to debunk Joan. In place of miraculous acts, he puts his belief in 'the evolutionary appetite', the driving force which can supersede man's common impulses and fill outstanding men and women with dynamic vigour. Joan's miraculous power consists in what she can make others do.

In the Preface, Shaw describes Joan as a 'born boss', and compares her skill as a commander to that of Napoleon and Nelson. This goes far beyond the assertions of the play, which makes few claims for Joan's powers as a military strategist. 'I welcome you as a saint, not as a soldier', Dunois, the true commander of the army, tells her before Orléans. This accords with the view of modern historians that Joan did not 'fight' in her battles. Dunois' common-sense approach to winning battles clearly has much to recommend it, and hindsight gives it the weight of truth:

I tell you as a soldier that God is no man's daily drudge, and no maid's either. If you are worthy of it he will sometimes snatch you out of the jaws of death and set you on your feet again . . . You must fight with all your might and all your craft . . . I tell you that your little hour of miracles is over, and that from this time on he who plays the war game best will win – if the luck is on his side.

Dunois is willing to learn the lessons of Agincourt, Poitiers and Crécy. He is a commander who can calculate ways and means, who feels great affection for Joan, but accuses her of lacking military professionalism:

Up to now she has had the numbers on her side; and she has won. But I know Joan; and I see that some day she will go ahead when she has only ten men to do the work of a hundred. And then she will find that God is on the side of the big battalions.

In the Epilogue, Joan asks Dunois if he has continued to fight in her way. In his reply, pragmatism again mingles with respect for her inspirational qualities: 'Faith it was any way that would win. But the way that won was always your way, I give you best, lassie.'

3.11 JOAN AND CHRIST

In her book *The Shavian Playground*, Margery Morgan refers to *Saint Joan* as a 'passion play'. There is much in Joan's role which is comparable to that of Christ. Both embarked upon a mission which took them from simple beginnings to a cruel public execution. Both had a revolutionary vision which exposed them to ecclesiastical doubts and jealousies.

Scene Five of Shaw's play, where the doomed heroine goes out to meet the people of Rheims, parallels the triumphs of Palm Sunday, so closely followed in the New Testament by the crucifixion. The desertion of Joan by her companions matches that of Christ by his disciples. Like Christ, Joan is 'bought', a fact underlined by the two references to Judas in Shaw's play. 'Wilt be a poor little Judas, and betray me and Him that sent me?', Joan asks the Dauphin in Scene Two. In Scene Six, after the execution, de Stogumber tells Ladvenu and Warwick: 'I am no better than Judas, I will hang myself'.

The trial itself, with Church and state conspiring to destroy Joan, recalls the activities of Romans and Jews in the New Testament. Like Pontius Pilate, Warwick, the civil power, gives responsibility to the spiritual authorities, only taking it back when the sentence is to be carried out.

The Epilogue, with de Stogumber (who has to see to believe) as Doubting Thomas, not only represents Joan's resurrection, but also raises questions which might equally well be applied to Christ. Shaw implies that Christ returned to Heaven at the Ascension because he too was faced with the problem expressed in Joan's closing lines: 'O God that madest this beautiful earth, when will it be ready to receive thy saints? How long, O Lord, how long?'

Shaw paints Joan and Christ as individuals from good backgrounds who were not especially ascetic. Both were cheerful figures, able to enjoy life. Shaw had little sympathy for the idea of Christ as the redeemer of men, and would have preferred to see him in a more political role. In the long Preface to *Androcles and the Lion* (1915) Shaw sadly noted that Jesus died not for his social and political opinions but because he believed himself to be the son of God. Had he been tried in a modern court he would have been sent to an asylum.

For Shaw, martyrdom was something to be avoided wherever possible. Lavinia, in *Androcles and the Lion* (1912) is about to face death as a Christian in a Roman arena. She insists that she is dying to assert her personal integrity, and for what she believes may be God: 'a man cannot die for a story and a dream'. Joan, even more clearly than Lavinia, sees that she would rather live than die. Only the threat of a life-time in an English prison finally tips the balance. In the Preface, Shaw asserts that neither Joan nor Christ were made significant merely through suffering. Their power, whether alive or dead, comes from their inherent genius. Both were agents of the Life Force.

After writing *Saint Joan*, Shaw contemplated a play about the trial of Christ, and he was still considering these issues when he wrote the Preface to his late play *On the Rocks* in 1933. There, he describes Christ as a 'communist':

> By every argument, legal, political, religious, customary, and polite, he was the most complete enemy of the society of his time ever brought to the bar. He was guilty on every count of the indictment, and on many more that his accusors had not the wit to frame. If he was innocent then the whole world was guilty.

In Shaw's eyes, Christ, like Joan, was a solitary figure, forced into isolation through his superiority to others. In each of the later scenes of *Saint Joan*, this loneliness is demonstrated, as society forces Joan out to a safe distance. At the end of Scene Five she says: 'My loneliness shall be my strength too; it is better to be alone with God'. The final image of the play is of Joan, left alone on the stage, an exile from the 'beautiful earth' which cannot accommodate her. She is powerless to effect any greater change. As a reformer, Joan, like Shaw's Christ, finally fails.

4 TECHNICAL FEATURES

4.1 THE STRUCTURE OF THE PLAY

Saint Joan is a play with six scenes and an Epilogue. Few of Shaw's plays are tightly constructed or 'well-made', and here he rejected the traditional form of the three or five act tragedy for what he called a 'chronicle play'. In an article written while he was at work on *Saint Joan* he explained what he meant:

> The cinema has restored to the stage the dramatic form used by Shakespear: the story told with utter disregard of the unity of place in a rapid succession of scenes, practically unlimited in number, uninterrupted by waits and just as short or as long as their dramatic interest can bear. In this free, varied, continuous manner, almost anyone who can tell a story well can also write a play. The specific ingenuity needed to force the story into the strait waistcoat of three or five acts, with one unchanging scene in each, is no longer needed.

Shakespeare's history plays provide Shaw with an apposite comparison; Joan of Arc is a character in *Henry VI: Part One*. Shaw was not, however, an admirer of Shakespeare, and he invokes his play as an example rather than source for his own. Shakespeare's Joan is a pasteboard figure, exemplifying English prejudices, and Shaw is rightly critical of the character in his *Saint Joan* Preface.

In his 'chronicle play', Shaw gives his scenes a correct historical progression. Going beyond Shakespeare, he specifies a precise location and often an exact date in his opening stage-directions. The first three all take place in the spring of 1429; Scene One at Vaucouleurs, Scene Two at Chinon on the late afternoon of 8 March, and Scene Three outside Orléans on 29 May. Scene Six is set on the morning of 30 May 1431, which was the actual day of Joan's execution. Even the Epilogue, one of the two scenes without historical basis, is dated to June 1456.

Again following chronicle tradition, Shaw includes scenes which vary in length. Scenes One, Two, Four, Five and the Epilogue are roughly equal, but Scene Three, set outside Orléans, is exceptionally short, while the trial scene, the climax of Shaw's play, is nearly twice as long as any other.

The central role enjoyed by Joan herself provides the play's chief unity. Like the protagonist of a picaresque or journey novel (e.g. Miguel de Cervantes' *Don Quixote* (1605-15) or Henry Fielding's *Joseph Andrews*, (1742), Joan's progression follows a linear rather than a circular course. Some major characters (Warwick, the Dauphin, Dunois, Cauchon, Stogumber) appear in more than one scene of her history, but others are presented in only one episode (de Baudricourt, de Poulengey, La Trémouille).

Shaw's choice of a structure associated with medieval mystery cycles and Renaissance history plays does not contradict the thoroughly modern tone of the play. Shaw's structure for *Saint Joan* is innovatory rather than old-fashioned, and looks forward to the theory of 'epic' drama propounded by the German Marxist writer, Bertolt Brecht. Brecht, who saw *Saint Joan* in the Berlin production directed by the great Austrian producer, Max Reinhardt (1873-1943), looked upon Shaw as a forerunner of his own development of political drama. He updated *Saint Joan* (together with *Major Barbara*) in his play *Saint Joan of the Stockyards* (1930) where Joan dies as the victim, not of Church and state, but of the ruthlessness of big business.

Brecht's development of 'epic' theatre resulted from a determination to make the audience think and act, rather than passively accept what was happening on the stage. In Brecht's view, the 'well-made play', where the parts related to the whole to produce a satisfying unity, encouraged complacency. His is a drama which presents historical events without regard for the unities of time and place. He faces the audience with the facts, and encourages them to draw the right conclusions from what they see. Shaw's hostile reaction to romantic plays about Joan of Arc allies him to Brecht who was determined not to send his audiences home with 'the cockles of their hearts warmed'.

At an early stage in writing *Saint Joan*, Shaw announced: 'I shall ignore the limitations of the nineteenth century scenic stage as completely as Shakespear did'. He wanted the play performed on an apron stage, not behind a proscenium arch. The scenery was to move behind while the action took place in front, and the effect would be like a circus or a lecture theatre. In the end, all that remained of this scheme was the projected slides of Joan's statues in the Epilogue. Neither of the opening productions of *Saint Joan* used an experimental set, nor do the very full stage directions for the published text suggest that Shaw finally envisaged a bare-stage technique. The 1983 production of the play at the National Theatre in London attempted a Brechtian approach, with processions and armies crossing between scenes. The effect, on the huge stage of the Olivier Theatre, was to dwarf the actors and muffle the debates. A more conventionally staged performance at the Belgrade Theatre, Coventry, also in 1983, was both more moving and more intellectually challenging. Shaw himself was fortunate in having an outstandingly talented designer for the first London production. The sets and costumes by Charles Ricketts (1866-1931) were described in one review as 'neither frankly representational nor uncompromisingly expressionistic, but a happy blend of the two.'

4.2 *SAINT JOAN* AS TRAGEDY

The 'chronicle' shape of *Saint Joan* is an unusual feature. It should, however, be recognised that there is much traditional tragedy in the play. Shaw himself rarely attempted to strike a note of 'high tragedy', but speaking of *Saint Joan* he said: 'What more do you want for a tragedy as great as that of Prometheus? All the forces that bring about the catastrophe are on the grandest scale and the individual soul on which they press is one of the most indomitable force and temper.' Like many great tragedies, Joan's is presented as unavoidable, a clash of giant forces. A note of foreboding is struck from the outset, and the audience's knowledge of the outcome results in a considerable degree of dramatic irony. An undertow of disaster underscores the comedy of the opening scenes, and gathers momentum as the play proceeds.

Without the Epilogue, the movement of the play approximates to the classical form of tragedy. The first three scenes, with their progressive upward movement, carry the heroine to her highest point, the relief of Orléans, which falls between Scenes Three and Four. Subsequent events take her downhill to her execution, a well defined pattern of tragic denouement. In Scene Five, Joan is accused by the Archbishop of the sin of pride, 'hubris', the tragic flaw of conventional drama. The Archbishop tells her: 'The old Greek tragedy is rising among us. It is the chastisement of hubris'. In the trial scene Joan herself accepts the judgement of pride when relating her capture to her insistence on wearing a gold surcoat.

Some critics take an entirely different line here. A few assert that a Christian play can never be a tragedy. Others see Shaw's introduction of the idea of pride as wholly ironic, an argument supported by those passages in the trial scene where Joan's accusors charge her with spiritual pride and vanity, their response to her ability to think for herself. A careful reading of Scene Five, however, does suggest that Joan is becoming over-confident and overweening, and there is, in that scene at least, some substance for the Archbishop's charge of 'hubris'.

The introduction of the Epilogue deliberately distorts any approximation to a recognisably tragic pattern. It inhibits the cathartic impulse of 'pity' and 'terror' declared by Aristotle to be essential to tragic drama. The horrifying fate of the heroine in Scene Six is now counteracted by her resurrection.

Shaw took up a provocative stance in defending the Epilogue in his Programme Note: 'Without it the play would be only a sensational tale of a girl who was burnt, leaving the spectators plunged into horror, despairing of humanity. The true tale of Saint Joan is a tale with a glorious ending; and any play that did not make this clear would be an insult to her memory.' In the Preface, Shaw is rather more honest about the actual effect of the Epilogue on an audience. He writes there of 'the comedy of the attempts of posterity to make amends for that execution'.

The Epilogue can perhaps be related to literary precedent in the nineteenth-century novel, rather than in drama. Visions of a future resolution often follow a tragic conclusion in Victorian fiction. One of the best examples is the end of the historical novel, *Tale of Two Cities*, published in 1859 by Charles Dickens (1812–70). At the end of the book, the hero, Sydney Carton, is executed on the guillotine during the French Revolution. He sacrifices his life to save others. As he mounts the steps of the platform, the narrator imagines what Carton's last vision might have been, carrying the reader forward into a peaceful future, both for France and for those whom Carton has saved. The effect is closer to Shaw's 'glorious ending' than the actual Epilogue to *Saint Joan*, which asserts a marked division between the slightly absurd canonisation of Joan, and the unchanging nature of human attitudes and behaviour. All the characters declare that if she came back to life Joan would have to die again. Shaw, unlike Dickens, does not project us into a better world, cleansed by the tragic sacrifices of the past.

4.3 CHARACTERISATION

Saint Joan, like other Shaw plays, contrasts the presentation of certain minor figures, with severely limited roles, with the far greater complexity of the major parts. Characters like de Baudricourt, the blustering bully; de La Trémouille, the bad-tempered power-seeker; or La Hire, the bluff soldier, belong to a recognisable theatrical tradition. They are incapable of surprising the audience. Such stock characters are appropriate to a 'chronicle play' which draws upon legends about Joan of Arc for much of its subject-matter, and their prototypes might be found in the pantomine. They are decisively introduced through the long and informative stage directions, and this, together with the equally clear-cut dialogue, leaves little room for an actor's personal interpretation.

Among the more fully represented roles are some which seem to have been created for purposes of dialectic and discussion, rather than for dramatic effect. The Inquisitor is a man ruled by the intellect, and, fascinated as we may be by his arguments, we have little sense of him as a human being. It is not altogether surprising to find Shaw on one occasion referring to him as 'a very amiable gentleman' and on another as 'a most infernal old scoundrel'.

Both Cauchon and Warwick are more than mouthpieces for the view of life which they represent. Warwick's delight in his book, and his relationship with his cheeky page, touch on the relaxed side of his worldliness. Desmond MacCarthy thought Warwick an eighteenth-century English aristocrat in manner, and his statements that the Jews give better value than the Christians, and that the Muhammadans were not as ill-bred as he had expected, could well have been uttered by any tolerant and civilised man of the world. Shaw made a practice of introducing Englishmen into his historical plays, most notably in *Caesar and Cleopatra*, where he greatly enjoys satirising twentieth-century English attitudes through Caesar's English secretary, Britannus. Here, in *Saint Joan*, Shaw seizes the opportunity offered by Warwick and de Stogumber, to present two different aspects of the Englishman abroad, the one who acclimatises himself, and the one who sticks out like a sore thumb.

Cauchon's fanatical attachment to the notion of an ideal Church gives little room for light relief in Shaw's characterisation. Cauchon's vision of a world in chaos and without leadership or order is a striking one for a modern audience, and particularly so far the post-war society of the 1920s. His lament at the desecration of his body brings Cauchon near to tragic status in the Epilogue, where his powerful use of emotive language rises to a moving climax.

Dunois is certainly the noblest male character in the play. This is the part for the leading man of the company. His handsome looks are made much of, but the romance with Joan which they might portend is ruled out, as much by Shaw's intention as by historical fact. Dunois consistently treats Joan as a woman, and irritates her by finding a womanly virtue in her love of babies. Joan's response, that all soldiers love babies, reveals a latent insecurity in this otherwise honestly matched relationship. Dunois admires Joan's courage, but, clear in his own judgement, puts a number of very important practical points to her. We have to accept that Dunois' arguments are perfectly valid, but we have also to ask ourselves whether his practical approach is not excessively limited. Shaw never answers the question, not even in Dunois' reappearance in the Epilogue.

Two characters in the play show themselves capable of change under the influence of Joan. The Dauphin's part provides an amusing and enjoyable acting role. Astute and intelligent, he only plays at being a fool, and his caution and rationality relate him to Shavian heroes like Caesar, or like Bluntschli in *Arms and the Man*. In his decision to accept Joan's mission in Scene Two, the Dauphin gives some indication of the fire which the heroine can breathe into others.

De Stogumber's change of heart in Scene Six is more dramatic and more lasting. From bigoted hatred of Joan, he is abruptly converted by his horror at her execution. Shaw believed that many of those who support violence would be similarly affected if actually confronted with what they had brought about.

De Stogumber's role is closely related to Joan's. They are the only two characters in the play able to enunciate strong beliefs without hesitation or worldly policy. In their polarisation of 'English' and

'French' both are committed nationalists. De Stogumber's change of heart, which turns him into a pleasant (if simple-minded) man, with a horror of violence, is simultaneous with Joan's execution, the event which accomplishes this change in him.

Shaw's inspiration to write his play was centred in his excitement over the role of Joan. His view of Joan as an historical figure has been discussed in Chapter 3, and we have seen how he rejected the 'plaster saint' image, and sought to make his Joan, with her rough language and her sturdy attitudes, into a valid and lively figure. His characterisation of Joan was deeply influenced both by his use of his sources and by his view of her as a pioneer in social, ecclesiastical and sexual matters.

Joan's radical spirit is expressed in the play through her lack of false respect for her 'superiors'. On her earlier appearances Joan presents a strong contrast to those who lack her clear beliefs and convictions. The power of her personality emerges in the first and second scenes through dialogues with de Baudricourt and the Dauphin, neither of whom is able to resist the force of her succinctly expressed argument.

In the later scenes of the play, Joan's bright and cheerful manner is modified by adversity, and the force of her will shows to less effect against characters whose belief in their calling is as strong as her own; Dunois, Cauchon, the Inquisitor. In Scene Five, Joan's modesty has almost deserted her, and Shaw suggests that her confidence in herself will lead to her downfall. Her bravery of spirit and unintellectual perspicacity in Scene Six and the Epilogue, however, ensure that the audience remain committed to this character to the end of the play.

In his own terms, Shaw was not entirely successful. The Joan story rouses certain in-built responses in an audience, however it is told. Shaw's comments on early productions of the play show how difficult it was for any actress to resist playing Joan as a saint rather than a superwoman.

Bernard Shaw's Joan has become one of the world's great acting roles. After sixty years, the freshness and vigour of the characterisation can still surprise and excite a theatre audience. Though Shaw would have detested the idea, Joan challenges comparison with Shakespeare's boy/girl heroines, Viola in *Twelfth Night* or Rosalind in *As You Like It*. Like them Joan has the clear-sightedness and vulnerability of youth, qualities which throw into relief the world-weary and grasping characters who surround her.

4.4 RHETORIC AND DEBATE

Shaw remained an experimental dramatist, playing games with theatrical expectations in order to unnerve his audience and to encourage them to think constructively. His greatest technical innovation was probably the introduction of intellectual debate into the theatre. Little happens in most of Shaw's plays, and his preference for characters who think and talk rather than act might easily render his dramas static and verbose.

Shaw avoids these dangers by using what appears to be colloquial and everyday speech. The dialogue of his plays is never obscure. There are no unfamiliar words or complicated patterns of imagery. As in the plays of Samuel Beckett or Harold Pinter, however, the simplicity is deceptive, and the language is far more artfully organised than at first appears. Like Pinter's, Shaw's dialogue is structured through repetition. In longer speeches he often employs a balanced and controlled sentence structure. T. S. Eliot grudgingly admitted that he might have been influenced by *Saint Joan* in his departure from verse and use of colloquial prose for the Knight's speeches in his historical play *Murder in the Cathedral* (1935). Like Shaw, Eliot was trying to make his audience consider an unpopular point of view, to articulate the possible reasoning of traditional 'villains'.

In several of his plays, Shaw introduces characters who seem to preach, an effect accentuated by the high level of reference both to the Bible and to the Anglican Book of Common Prayer. From the service of Morning Prayer comes the Latin hymn, the Te Deum, which Shaw adapts as a hymn of praise to Joan in the Epilogue. Shaw's adaptations of original sources are often very revealing. When Joan says: 'Though men have destroyed my body, yet in my soul I have seen God', she is echoing the book of Job, Chapter 19, verse 26. Shaw was probably more familiar with Handel's setting of this particular line in the *Messiah* (1741). 'Tho' worms destroy this body, yet in my flesh shall I see God'. Shaw's two changes to the original, 'men' for 'worms' and 'soul' for 'flesh', underline two points in the Epilogue. Joan's destroyer is not the natural one, worms and corruption, but her fellow men. Dead, she has seen God, but not in her flesh. Her soul has become the only resting place for a solitary saint.

There are extended passages of debate throughout *Saint Joan*, but Scene Four and the earlier part of Scene Six can be singled out as notable examples. The Inquisitor's speech, which requires a good deal of attention from the audience, can last for six or seven minutes. One reason for its success is its shock value. An Anglo-Saxon audience does not expect to hear a plausible defence of the Inquisition presented by a reasonable and apparently kindly man.

Critics have referred to the symphonic effect of Scene Four, where Cauchon and Warwick play the main themes, and de Stogumber's abruptness acts as a restatement in a different key. Shaw often uses simple characters like Stogumber and Ladvenu to stimulate and refocus the debate among the intellectuals. They are sincere men who speak from the heart, and their directness, like Joan's, cuts across the smooth sentences of practised rhetoricians. To a lesser extent, the three pages who appear in different scenes of the play perform a similar function, in their case by introducing an element of frivolity and gaiety into what are otherwise serious occasions.

Joan herself rarely speaks at length, an unusual characteristic in a Shavian protagonist. When she does rise to lyricism, in the long speech just before she dies, Joan also moves into an uncharacteristic series of negatives and subjunctives, 'no', 'never', 'without', 'cannot', are the dominating words as she rejects a life without freedom and joy.

4.5 HUMOUR

So entrenched was Shaw's reputation for finding mirth in what others regarded as serious, that one reviewer of the first English production professed great relief that the dramatist had not held his heroine up to ridicule. Shaw's own comments show that he did indeed find some humour in the original story. Joan's own irony, as it comes across in the records, attracted him, while the burning of Joan, being a 'judicial' and 'pious' murder brought an 'element of comedy into the tragedy'.

There is much gaiety in *Saint Joan*, the pantomime scene with de Baudricourt, for example, or the gentler merriment of Dunois' dialogue with his page in Scene Three. Other passages juxtapose humour with seriousness in the manner of the gravedigger scene from *Hamlet*, sharpening the effect of a poignant moment. The outstanding example of this is the trial scene. Absurd arguments about the language and dress of saints even make the characters laugh, and de Stogumber's obsessive interjections about the Bishop of Senlis' horse smack of pure farce. If de Stogumber instigates much laughter, however, his vindictiveness and malice can never be forgotten.

Shaw's most effective comedy often comes in single lines of repartee. The deflating effect of anachronism provides him with some of his wittiest moments. When the Dauphin tells Joan: 'you may spare your breath to cool your porridge', or when he greets her intended return to Domrémy with 'that will be very nice', the juxtaposition of a pithy colloquialism, or of a vacuous modern cliché with the crusading mission of a medieval saint is bound to evoke laughter. Shaw had already used the first expression to good effect in *Caesar and Cleopatra*, making his confrontation of two worlds humorous as well as striking.

There are numerous examples of this device throughout the play. Many of the best are given to Charles, but the greeting between Joan and Warwick in the Epilogue is particularly delightful. Here both use the meaningless language of twentieth-century polite society, when their subject is not a social embarrassment, but the burning of one at the command of the other:

> WARWICK. Madam: my congratulations on your rehabilitation. I feel that I owe you an apology.
> JOAN. Oh, please dont mention it.

One reviewer believed that Shaw found writing the Epilogue a relief after the unwelcome seriousness of Scene Six. The introduction of Cauchon prevents the Epilogue from becoming merely amusing, but there is much ridicule of sacred things. The soldier finds his day away from 'jolly' hell very boring; the Dauphin and Dunois, comic versions of Christ's apostles in Gethsemane, cannot stay awake and slip off to bed; Stogumber, who has devoted his life to Joan's memory, insists that her ghost is someone else. The messenger from the Vatican is a pompous bore, whose jargon parodies the bureaucratic purveyors of red tape: 'The possibility of your resurrection was not contemplated in the recent proceedings for your canonization. I must return to Rome for fresh instructions.'

Such humour is modern rather than medieval, but Shaw did allow himself a few jibes at the more absurd aspects of fifteenth-century behaviour. Charles tells his court that there is a family tradition of having a private saint. His grandfather's levitated, and his father went one better and had two. La Hire amusingly illustrates the wide division between language and religious truth, the way in which notions of heaven and hell had become trivialised. He declares that 'If ever I utter an oath again may my soul be blasted to eternal damnation!', and starts another sentence 'by all the devils in hell', rapidly substituting 'by Our Lady and all the saints', when he realises what he has said.

4.6 STAGE DIRECTIONS

Shaw's long stage directions are proverbial. The printed texts of his plays sold in immense numbers, and Shaw no doubt intended these directions for readers rather than for actors or stage-managers. Even so, they make it clear that Shaw had exact ideas about certain features of his plays. In the opening direction of each scene Shaw gives a precise account of the setting, the placing of furniture, windows and doors. In Scene Three he describes the long expanse of the River Loire laid out behind the action. Elsewhere, Shaw draws particular attention to medieval details, a thirteenth-century window at Vaucouleurs, curtained walls and a votive picture of the Virgin in the royal castle of the Epilogue.

As each of the major characters comes on to the stage, Shaw's direction gives a very exact facial description. No actor could hope to do more than roughly approximate to Shaw's ideal. Shaw had been looking at portraits of Charles VII: and physiognomy becomes a clue to character when the Dauphin enters: 'He has little narrow eyes, near together, a long pendulous nose that droops over his thick short upper lip, and the expression of a young dog accustomed to be kicked.' For the description of Joan herself, with wide-spaced eyes, and strong features, Shaw drew upon the sculptured head in Orleans, which was once thought to be Joan and which he mentions in the Preface.

The short directions which follow the characters' names in the text tell the actors how the speech should sound, while the longer directions tell them what to do on stage, even, on occasion, giving brief additional details about them. In Gilles de Rais's case the future emerges when Shaw tells us that Gilles was to be hanged eleven years later. Other important directions give clues to the balance of the dialogue, as when Shaw notes that Warwick seemingly defers to Cauchon in Scene Four, but that he leads the discussion and expects to dominate.

The overall effect of Shaw's directions is restrictive. They should perhaps be seen as predominantly for readers, but if they were followed exactly on stage, actors would have little room for personal interpretation. It is as though Shaw has no wish to allow performance of his play to pass out of his own grasp. Like the Preface, the instructions provide us with another set of rules for interpreting the play.

5 CRITICAL ANALYSIS OF A SELECTED PASSAGE

5.1 PASSAGE (SCENE TWO)

CHARLES. We shall see. I am not such a fool as I look. I have my eyes open; and I can tell you that one good treaty is worth ten good fights. These fighting fellows lose all on the treaties that they gain on the fights. If we can only have a treaty, the English are sure to have the worst of it, because they are better at fighting than at thinking.

JOAN. If the English win, it is they that will make the treaty; and then God help poor France! Thou must fight, Charlie, whether thou will or no. I will go first to hearten thee. We must take our courage in both hands': aye, and pray for it with both hands too.

CHARLES. [*descending from his throne and again crossing the room to escape from her dominating urgency*] Oh do stop talking about God and praying. I cant bear people who are always praying. Isnt it bad enough to have to do it at the proper times?

JOAN. [*pitying him*] Thou poor child, thou hast never prayed in thy life. I must teach thee from the beginning.

CHARLES. I am not a child: I am a grown man and a father; and I will not be taught any more.

JOAN. Aye, you have a little son. He that will be Louis the Eleventh when you die. Would you not fight for him?

CHARLES. No: a horrid boy. He hates me. He hates everybody, selfish little beast! I dont want to be bothered with children. I dont want to be a father; and I dont want to be a son: especially a son of St Louis. I dont want to be any of these fine things you all have your heads full of: I want to be just what I am. Why cant you mind your own business, and let me mind mine?

JOAN, [*again contemptuous*] Minding your own business is like minding your own body: it's the shortest way to make yourself sick. What is my business? Helping mother at home. What is thine? Petting lapdogs and sucking sugar-sticks. I call that muck. I tell thee it is God's business we are here to do: not our own. I have a message to thee from God; and thou must listen to it, though thy heart break with the terror of it.

CHARLES. I dont want a message; but can you tell me any secrets? Can you do any cures? Can you turn lead into gold, or anything of that sort?

JOAN. I can turn thee into a king, in Rheims Cathedral; and that is a miracle that will take some doing, it seems.

CHARLES. If we go to Rheims, and have a coronation, Anne will want new dresses. We cant afford them. I am all right as I am.

JOAN. As you are! And what is that? Less than my father's poorest shepherd. Thourt not lawful owner of thy own land of France till thou be consecrated.

CHARLES. But I shall not be lawful owner of my own land anyhow. Will the consecration pay off my mortgages? I have pledged my last acre to the Archbishop and that fat bully. I owe money even to Bluebeard.

JOAN. [*earnestly*] Charlie: I come from the land, and have gotten my strength working on the land; and I tell thee that the land is thine to rule righteously and keep God's peace in, and not to pledge at the pawnshop as a drunken woman pledges her children's clothes. And I come from God to tell thee to kneel in the cathedral and solemnly give thy kingdom to Him for ever and ever, and become the greatest king in the world as His steward and His bailiff, His soldier and His servant. The very clay of France will become holy: her soldiers will be the soldiers of God: the rebel dukes will be rebels against God: the English will fall on their knees and beg thee let them return to their lawful homes in peace. Wilt be a poor little Judas, and betray me and Him that sent me?

CHARLES. [*tempted at last*] Oh, if I only dare!

JOAN. I shall dare, dare, and dare again, in God's name! Art for or against me?

CHARLES. [*excited*] I'll risk it. I warn you I shant be able to keep it up; but I'll risk it. You shall see.

5.2 COMMENTARY

This passage comes from the later part of Scene Two of *Saint Joan* where Joan has her first private conversation with the Dauphin Charles. Joan persuades him to let her take charge of the army, in order to lead an assault and relieve Orléans. At the end of the passage, Charles calls back the court to tell them of his decision in her favour.

This is a passage in which stronger overwhelms weaker as Joan makes Charles an instrument of her own power. The dialogue is one of two in the play where Joan, through sheer force of personality, wins over a doubting listener whose assistance she needs in order to fulfil her mission. The other such dialogue is her victory over de Baudricourt in Scene One. Later in the play she comes up against opponents as convinced as herself (most notably Cauchon) and is, as a result, unable to exercise her force of personality.

At the opening of this passage, the Dauphin, at Joan's request, is sitting on his throne towards the back of the stage. The gap between the conventional image of an enthroned king and Charles's actual appearance is important. Shaw has told us in an earlier stage direction that the Dauphin is of a gentle and unimpressive appearance, something accentuated by an ugly hat which covers all his hair.

The sturdy and determined Joan presents a strong contrast to him, and this is accentuated by their different manner of speech, he petulant and uncertain, she committed and direct. After a few lines, Joan's aggression drives Charles from the throne, and we may imagine him moving nervously about the throne room as Joan tries to pin him down.

The dialogue is dominated by the repetition of words and phrases, a rhetorical device employed by both speakers. Charles's opening speech revolves around the balancing of two contrasting nouns: 'treaty' and 'fight', which he uses in order to prove to Joan that, as the English are better at fighting than treaties, a treaty is a more effective weapon against them than a fight. The balance of 'treaty' and 'fight' is matched by that of other terms: 'lose' and 'gain'; 'fighting' and 'thinking'; 'English' and 'French'.

Joan then takes up the same nouns in her turn, in order to counter Charles's argument with one of her own: that the side which wins the fight will make the treaty. As the dialogue continues, the speakers echo a word from the previous speech. This interplay gives the effect of genuine argument and discussion between the two. Above all, it implies that each is listening to the other, and commenting directly on the other's statements. Joan advises Charles to pray. Charles says that he hates praying. Joan calls Charles a child, he denies it. Charles says that he wants to mind his own business, and Joan tells him that he must do God's business. Here the words 'minding' and 'business' are intertwined like 'treaty' and 'fight' so that the prose of the speakers is again deliberately patterned and organised.

Just as Charles is giving way, Joan utters the strongest line in the passage, again using the reinforcement of repetition. 'I shall dare, dare, and dare again, in God's name!' This is the line which she repeats at the end of Scene Five, where it is adapted to look forward to her approaching death: 'In His strength I will dare, and dare, and dare, until I die'.

Throughout her discussion with the Dauphin, Joan is stating the positive case, Charles the negative. His lines begin with such expressions as 'I am not' (twice); 'do stop talking'; 'No'; 'I dont want' (four times in gradually rising crescendo); 'I shall not be lawful owner'. In face of this, Joan makes a series of positive statements interspersed with commands; 'Thou must' (twice): 'I will'; 'We must'; 'I must'; 'Aye'; 'I can'.

The low and materialistic level of Charles's expectation is shown in his hope that Joan can turn lead into gold, and her mixture of strength and humour in her reply: 'I can turn thee into a king, in Rheims cathedral; and that is a miracle that will take some doing, it seems'. For Charles, the coronation means, not a religious consecration, but new clothes for his wife: 'We cant afford them.'

Shaw's idiosyncratic mixture of modern and rustic language is particularly marked in this passage. Joan consistently uses old-fashioned forms of verbs: 'hast'; 'though thy heart break'; 'He that will be Louis the Eleventh'; 'Thourt'; 'gotten'; 'Wilt' as well as 'thee'; 'thou' and 'thine'. Other expressions are contemporary with the date of the play, not with Joan of Arc, as when Joan tells Charles that the land is his to rule properly 'and not to pledge at the pawnshop as a drunken woman pledges her children's clothes'. Early critics objected to Joan calling the Dauphin 'Charlie', and one reviewer thought that 'I call that muck' made her sound like a girl from Oldham, not Domrémy.

Charles's speech is much more consistently modern, as it is throughout the play. He calls his son 'a horrid boy', and 'selfish little beast', describes his commanders as 'Those fighting fellows', and asks whether the consecration will pay off his mortgages.

Certain lines in the passage relate to Shaw's wider interests in *Saint*

Joan. Joan's statement that her business is helping her 'mother at home' and that Charles's business is 'petting lapdogs and sucking sugar-sticks' equates the two activities, the woman's and the idle king's, as 'muck'. God's business will release them both from such triviality, incidentally giving Joan a reason for superseding the despised feminine role.

Joan's reference to 'my father's poorest shepherd' reminds us of Shaw's insistence that Joan is a bourgeoise not a peasant, implied here through the reminder that her father employs others to guard his sheep.

Shaw was not above displaying his historical knowledge. Lest his audience should forget that Charles VII was the father of the unpleasant 'spider king' Louis XI, well known to English-speaking readers from Sir Walter Scott's *Quentin Durward* (1823), Joan tells us: 'He that will be Louis the Eleventh when you die'. This gives Charles the chance to give a foretaste of his five-year-old son's reputation.

Joan finally wins the argument with one of her few long speeches. She tells the Dauphin that he is merely God's vice-gerent, 'His steward and His bailiff, His soldier and His servant'. Charles must carry out his responsibilities. Joan's language takes on a religious fervour as she balances the 'soldiers of God', the French, against the 'rebels against God', the rebel dukes. The prose rises to a climax with such expressions as 'keep God's peace'; 'The very clay of France will become holy'; 'solemnly give thy kingdom to Him for ever and ever'; with its echo of the Lord's Prayer ('for thine is the kingdom, the power, and the glory, For ever and ever').

Joan's vision here is not fulfilled in the later scenes of the play. Charles's comments on his coronation in Scene Six show us how far he falls short of proper solemnity on that occasion. In failing to rescue Joan after her capture, he becomes the Judas she fears, and fulfils his own warning that he will not 'be able to keep it up'. Characteristically, Shaw suggests the end of Joan's story, even when it is only beginning.

6 CRITICAL RECEPTION

6.1 THE EARLY REVIEWS AND COMMENTARIES

Saint Joan is widely regarded as the crowning achievement of Shaw's career, the play which finally established him in the public mind as a major dramatist. The original reviews were mixed and even hostile, but it was soon apparent that Shaw had achieved a great popular success. *Saint Joan* ran for over two hundred performances in both New York and London.

Understandably, with an author in his sixties, several theatre critics judged the play according to existing preconceptions about Shaw. Jeanne Foster in the *Transatlantic Review* referred to *Saint Joan* as 'tedious and loquacious, a mere historical scaffolding upon which the dramatist drapes the old Shavian gonfalons of wit and skilful lampoonery. Many critics have praised the play but a few have been honest and cried loudly like wise children: "The king is naked".'

In London, A. B. Walkley, the drama critic of *The Times*, condemned *Saint Joan* in advance without having seen or read it. He argued that Joan's story was not a fitting subject for Shaw's flippancy and iconoclasm. After the first performance, Walkley climbed down:

We think the play one of Mr. Shaw's finest achievements . . . When all is said . . . the great figure of the story remains a lovely thing, lovely in simplicity, lovely in faith. There are no heroics; only a little limelight now and then, which no one will grudge her.

Walkley's review was not without strictures. He regretted Shaw's insistence on 'dragging' in the present day, as well as his undramatic concern with fidelity to his sources, and with 'historical exegesis'. Above all, Walkley condemned the Epilogue: Mr. Shaw, having kept himself in hand for six scenes, let himself go in the last'.

Criticism of the Epilogue was almost universal among reviewers and commentators, particularly those who had seen the London production. Most felt that the Epilogue was repetitive and redundant, that it merely underlined what was implicit in the play. Alexander Woolcott, writing for the *New York Herald*, was one of the few who discerned Shaw's own intention:

> It is as though Shaw were to step out into the audience and shake the fat fellow in the front row whom the play had worked up into such a glow of sympathy, such a flutter of easy pity – shake him and whisper in his ear: 'If you had been in Rouen that day are you sure you would not have voted with the Bishop of Beauvais and run with the witch-burning mob to see the torch applied!

Attacks on the Epilogue can be associated with two consistent features of Shaw criticism: that his plays are too long, and that they are dominated by discussion rather than action. At the time of the first American production of *Saint Joan* in 1923 the Theater Guild asked Shaw's permission to make cuts in Scene Four and in the earlier part of Scene Six, both sections in which Joan does not appear. Shaw who claimed that he had already cut the play by a third before submitting it to them, refused, and the cuts were not made. Later, Shaw put his case in an essay, adapted for inclusion in the Preface. He surmised that the effect of the proposed cuts would be balanced by the Company's addition of more spectacular material, probably scenes at Orléans and Rheims, which would completely transform the play and make it into just another account of a popular heroine.

Opinions varied on the effect of Scene Four. The anonymous critic of the *Stage* (reviewing the New York production) said it was 'the old Shaw at his best', but the German novelist, Thomas Mann (1875–1955), thought it an 'unhappy scrambling of essay and drama'. Herbert Griffith in the *Observer* declared that 'I, and I think the audience, was interested in one thing only, Joan'. Griffith believed that the trial scene should have been extended and made into two: 'But there is only one trial scene, and half of this is the theology of Bishop Cauchon'.

The complaint that Joan herself was not sufficiently prominent was echoed by James Agate in *The Sunday Times*. While pretending not to do so, he regretted the absence of the familiar episodes in the Joan legend. Agate felt that the play might have opened in the fields of Domrémy and included the coronation scene at Rheims, instead of fobbing the audience 'off with the less important cloisters, and what for a time looks like mere desultory chatter'.

The American critic, Edmund Wilson, came closest to seeing the play as Shaw intended. For Wilson, 'Most of the really thrilling passages are those in which we feel the great forces of human history at work', Scenes Four and Six. Wilson continued:

> I do not see how those critics who have objected to the Epilogue can really understand what the play is about: if the Epilogue were to go, the tent scene would have to go too – as would also the Inquisitor's speech and a good deal more; we should, in fact, have to have a different play built on different lines, and with Joan's individual tragedy and not human history as its theme.

Even Wilson accused Shaw of 'prolixity' and over-explicitness, of making his characters improbably aware of their own historical role. Wilson takes Joan's statement that her voices come from her imagination in Scene One as 'disconcertingly out of key with the naïve faith of the middle ages'.

Historians criticised Shaw for the same reasons. J. M. Robertson attacked him for his historical inaccuracy and for failing to understand the middle ages in *Mr Shaw and 'The Maid'* of 1925; and in the same year the Dutch historian, Johan Huizinga, made a more moderate and appreciative statement of the same arguments in 'Bernard Shaw's Saint'. Huizinga took exception to Shaw's use of the terms 'Protestantism' and 'Nationalism', seeing the former as anachronistic in this context, and the latter as out-of-date, since nationalism was already well established in England and well on the way to being so in France.

Saint Joan was first performed in Paris in 1925, directed by George and Ludmilla Pitoëff, with Ludmilla in the leading role. It was an overwhelming success. French anxiety that Shaw might attack a French saint was defused by the performance, which remained in the Pitoëffs' repertoire for many years. French critics were more concerned with the play's quality as art than with its ideas, quite unlike their counterparts in Britain and America. Shaw himself disapproved of the Pitoëffs' production, which relied heavily on the emotional force of Ludmilla Pitoëff's acting. He told her that she had given too much weight to the presentation of the heroine. In defiance of Shaw, the Pitoëffs had presented the play as the English critics would have wanted it – as a tragic play about a martyred saint.

6.2 LATER STANDING OF *SAINT JOAN*

In 1924, Desmond MacCarthy described *Saint Joan* as 'probably I think, the greatest of Shaw's plays'. Not all later critics have placed *Saint Joan* right at the top, but the play has maintained a very high reputation among Shaw's oeuvre. In our own day, *Heartbreak House* is perhaps more frequently reckoned to be the author's masterpiece, but *Saint Joan* is still his most performed work. It has been seen in theatres all over the world, and among well-known actresses who have played the part in recent years are Joan Plowright, Janet Suzman and Frances de la Tour.

In 1936, Shaw himself was involved in a scheme to film *Saint Joan*, with the Austrian actress, Elizabeth Bergner, in the leading role. The plan aroused the Catholic Action Group in the United States to object to the play as 'essentially damaging'. In a letter to the *New York Times* Shaw advanced the counter-argument that his play was doing a service to the Catholic Church. It endorsed the verdict of the canonisation, not that of the condemnation, which Catholic Action seemed by contrast to be supporting. The film was never made.

Otto Preminger's film of 1957, starring Jean Seberg, used a version of Shaw's play adapted for the screen by Graham Greene. It was, surprisingly, a box-office disaster.

REVISION QUESTIONS

1. Can Shaw's Joan be described as a tragic heroine?
2. Consider some of the ways in which Shaw compares Joan to Christ.
3. How does Shaw define the 'miraculous' in *Saint Joan*?
4. By what means does Shaw convey Joan's special quality as an agent of 'creative evolution'?
5. Does the play substantiate Shaw's claim that Joan was a pioneer feminist?
6. Shaw deliberately omitted certain episodes traditionally associated with Joan of Arc from his play. Why do you think he did so, and what is the effect of the omissions?
7. Comment on some of the ways in which Shaw uses the language and appearance of his characters to underline their personalities and their role.
8. Shaw believed that Joan's trial was fairly conducted. How does he set out to make the audience share this belief, and does he succeed?
9. Illustrate some of the ways in which Shaw makes the discussion of ideas dramatically effective.
10. The trial scene is generally regarded as the climax of Shaw's play. Do you agree with this opinion?
11. What is the function of Scene Four in the overall scheme of the play?
12. Why do you think that some productions of *Saint Joan* omit the Epilogue? What is lost through such an omission?
13. How would you define Saint Joan's particular quality as a history play?

14. Why are ideas of 'nationalism' and 'protestantism' so important to *Saint Joan*?

15. By what means did Shaw set out to shake a theatre audience out of its complacency?

16. Shaw called his play a 'chronicle play'. What do you think that he meant by this expression?

17. Shaw accused his predecessors of not understanding the Middle Ages. How effectively does he evoke the medieval period in *Saint Joan*?

18. How does Shaw introduce ideas of social and political change into *Saint Joan*?

19. How would you characterise the humour of *Saint Joan*?

FURTHER READING

Saint Joan is published in paperback form by both Penguin Books and Longman's Study Texts Series. The Penguin is a plain text, while the Longman edition has an introduction and a range of notes.

T. F. Evans (ed.), *Shaw: the Critical Heritage* (London: Routledge, 1976). Reviews of *Saint Joan* are reprinted pp. 276–95.

A. Henderson, *Bernard Shaw: Playboy and Prophet* (London: D. Appleton, 1932). Reprints Shaw's 'Programme Note' to *Saint Joan*, pp. 545–7.

M. Meisel, *Shaw and the Nineteenth-Century Theater* (Princeton University Press, 1963).

D. MacCarthy, *Shaw* (London: MacGibbon and Kee, 1951).

M. M. Morgan, *The Shavian Playground* (London: Methuen, 1972).

T. Douglas Murray, *Jeanne D'Arc: Maid of Orléans* (London: Heinemann, 1902).

R. N. Roy, *George Bernard Shaw's Historical Plays* (Delhi: Macmillan Company of India, 1976).

E. Sprigge, *Sybil Thorndike Casson* (London: Gollancz, 1971).

M. Warner, *Joan of Arc: The Image of Female Heroism* (London: Weidenfeld, 1981).

S. Weintraub, *Saint Joan: Fifty Years After* (Baton Rouge, Louisiana State University Press, 1973). A collection of reviews and articles about *Saint Joan*.

J. L. Wisenthal, *The Marriage of Contraries: Bernard Shaw's Middle Plays* (Harvard University Press, Cambridge, Mass., 1974).

Mastering English Literature
Richard Gill

Mastering English Literature will help readers both to enjoy English Literature and to be successful in 'O' levels, 'A' levels and other public exams. It is an introduction to the study of poetry, novels and drama which helps the reader in four ways - by providing ways of approaching literature, by giving examples and practice exercises, by offering hints on how to write about literature, and by the author's own evident enthusiasm for the subject. With extracts from more than 200 texts, this is an enjoyable account of how to get the maximum satisfaction out of reading, whether it be for formal examinations or simply for pleasure.

Work Out English Literature ('A' level)
S.H. Burton

This book familiarises 'A' level English Literature candidates with every kind of test which they are likely to encounter. Suggested answers are worked out step by step and accompanied by full author's commentary. The book helps students to clarify their aims and establish techniques and standards so that they can make appropriate responses to similar questions when the examination pressures are on. It opens up fresh ways of looking at the full range of set texts, authors and critical judgements and motivates students to know more of these matters.

THE MACMILLAN SHAKESPEARE

General Editor: PETER HOLLINDALE
Advisory Editor: PHILIP BROCKBANK

The Macmillan Shakespeare features:
* clear and uncluttered texts with modernised punctuation and spelling wherever possible;
* full explanatory notes printed on the page facing the relevant text for ease of reference;
* stimulating introductions which concentrate on content, dramatic effect, character and imagery, rather than mere dates and sources.

Above all, The Macmillan Shakespeare treats each play as a work for the theatre which can also be enjoyed on the page.

CORIOLANUS
Editor: Tony Parr

THE WINTER'S TALE
Editor: Christopher Parry

MUCH ADO ABOUT NOTHING
Editor: Jan McKeith

RICHARD II
Editor: Richard Adams

RICHARD III
Editor: Richard Adams

HENRY IV, PART I
Editor: Peter Hollindale

HENRY IV, PART II
Editor: Tony Parr

HENRY V
Editor: Brian Phythian

AS YOU LIKE IT
Editor: Peter Hollindale

A MIDSUMMER NIGHT'S DREAM
Editor: Norman Sanders

THE MERCHANT OF VENICE
Editor: Christopher Parry

THE TAMING OF THE SHREW
Editor: Robin Hood

TWELFTH NIGHT
Editor: E. A. J. Honigmann

THE TEMPEST
Editor: A. C. Spearing

ROMEO AND JULIET
Editor: James Gibson

JULIUS CAESAR
Editor: D. R. Elloway

MACBETH
Editor: D. R. Elloway

HAMLET
Editor: Nigel Alexander

ANTONY AND CLEOPATRA
Editors: Jan McKeith and
Richard Adams

OTHELLO
Editors: Celia Hilton and R. T. Jones

KING LEAR
Editor: Philip Edwards

MACMILLAN STUDENTS' NOVELS

General Editor: JAMES GIBSON

The Macmillan Students' Novels are low-priced, new editions of major classics, aimed at the first examination candidate. Each volume contains:

* enough explanation and background material to make the novels accessible — and rewarding — to pupils with little or no previous knowledge of the author or the literary period;

* detailed notes elucidate matters of vocabulary, interpretation and historical background;

* eight pages of plates comprising facsimiles of manuscripts and early editions, portraits of the author and photographs of the geographical setting of the novels.

JANE AUSTEN: MANSFIELD PARK
Editor: Richard Wirdnam

JANE AUSTEN: NORTHANGER ABBEY
Editor: Raymond Wilson

JANE AUSTEN: PRIDE AND PREJUDICE
Editor: Raymond Wilson

JANE AUSTEN: SENSE AND SENSIBILITY
Editor: Raymond Wilson

JANE AUSTEN: PERSUASION
Editor: Richard Wirdnam

CHARLOTTE BRONTË: JANE EYRE
Editor: F. B. Pinion

EMILY BRONTË: WUTHERING HEIGHTS
Editor: Graham Handley

JOSEPH CONRAD: LORD JIM
Editor: Peter Hollindale

CHARLES DICKENS: GREAT EXPECTATIONS
Editor: James Gibson

CHARLES DICKENS: HARD TIMES
Editor: James Gibson

CHARLES DICKENS: OLIVER TWIST
Editor: Guy Williams

CHARLES DICKENS: A TALE OF TWO CITIES
Editor: James Gibson

GEORGE ELIOT: SILAS MARNER
Editor: Norman Howlings

GEORGE ELIOT: THE MILL ON THE FLOSS
Editor: Graham Handley

D. H. LAWRENCE: SONS AND LOVERS
Editor: James Gibson

D. H. LAWRENCE: THE RAINBOW
Editor: James Gibson

MARK TWAIN: HUCKLEBERRY FINN
Editor: Christopher Parry

Also from Macmillan

CASEBOOK SERIES

The Macmillan *Casebook* series brings together the best of modern criticism with a selection of early reviews and comments. Each Casebook charts the development of opinion on a play, poem, or novel, or on a literary genre, from its first appearance to the present day.

GENERAL THEMES

COMEDY: DEVELOPMENTS IN
CRITICISM
D. J. Palmer

DRAMA CRITICISM:
DEVELOPMENTS SINCE IBSEN
A. J. Hinchliffe

THE ENGLISH NOVEL:
DEVELOPMENTS IN CRITICISM
SINCE HENRY JAMES
Stephen Hazell

THE LANGUAGE OF LITERATURE
N. Page

THE PASTORAL MODE
Bryan Loughrey

THE ROMANTIC IMAGINATION
J. S. Hill

TRAGEDY: DEVELOPMENTS IN
CRITICISM
R. P. Draper

POETRY

WILLIAM BLAKE: SONGS OF
INNOCENCE AND EXPERIENCE
Margaret Bottrall

BROWNING: MEN AND WOMEN
AND OTHER POEMS
J. R. Watson

BYRON: CHILDE HAROLD'S
PILGRIMAGE AND DON JUAN
John Jump

CHAUCER: THE CANTERBURY
TALES
J. J. Anderson

COLERIDGE: THE ANCIENT
MARINER AND OTHER POEMS
A. R. Jones and W. Tydeman

DONNE: SONGS AND SONETS
Julian Lovelock

T. S. ELIOT: FOUR QUARTETS
Bernard Bergonzi

T. S. ELIOT: PRUFROCK,
GERONTION, ASH WEDNESDAY
AND OTHER POEMS
B. C. Southam

T. S. ELIOT: THE WASTELAND
C. B. Cox and A. J. Hinchliffe

ELIZABETHAN POETRY: LYRICAL
AND NARRATIVE
Gerald Hammond

THOMAS HARDY: POEMS
J. Gibson and T. Johnson

GERALD MANLEY HOPKINS:
POEMS
Margaret Bottrall

KEATS: ODES
G. S. Fraser

KEATS: THE NARRATIVE POEMS
J. S. Hill

MARVELL: POEMS
Arthur Pollard

THE METAPHYSICAL POETS
Gerald Hammond

MILTON: PARADISE LOST
A. E. Dyson and Julian Lovelock

POETRY OF THE FIRST WORLD
WAR
Dominic Hibberd

ALEXANDER POPE: THE RAPE OF
THE LOCK
John Dixon Hunt

SHELLEY: SHORTER POEMS &
LYRICS
Patrick Swinden

SPENSER: THE FAERIE QUEEN
Peter Bayley

TENNYSON: IN MEMORIAM
John Dixon Hunt

THIRTIES POETS: 'THE AUDEN
GROUP'
Ronald Carter

WORDSWORTH: LYRICAL
BALLADS
A. R. Jones and W. Tydeman

WORDSWORTH: THE PRELUDE
W. J. Harvey and R. Gravil

W. B. YEATS: POEMS 1919–1935
E. Cullingford

W. B. YEATS: LAST POEMS
Jon Stallworthy

THE NOVEL AND PROSE

JANE AUSTEN: EMMA
David Lodge

JANE AUSTEN: NORTHANGER
ABBEY AND PERSUASION
B. C. Southam

JANE AUSTEN: SENSE AND
SENSIBILITY, PRIDE AND
PREJUDICE AND MANSFIELD
PARK
B. C. Southam

CHARLOTTE BRONTË: JANE EYRE
AND VILLETTE
Miriam Allott

EMILY BRONTË: WUTHERING
HEIGHTS
Miriam Allott

BUNYAN: THE PILGRIM'S
PROGRESS
R. Sharrock

CONRAD: HEART OF DARKNESS,
NOSTROMO AND UNDER
WESTERN EYES
C. B. Cox

CONRAD: THE SECRET AGENT
Ian Watt

CHARLES DICKENS: BLEAK
HOUSE
A. E. Dyson

CHARLES DICKENS: DOMBEY
AND SON AND LITTLE DORRITT
Alan Shelston

CHARLES DICKENS: HARD TIMES,
GREAT EXPECTATIONS AND OUR
MUTUAL FRIEND
N. Page

GEORGE ELIOT: MIDDLEMARCH
Patrick Swinden

GEORGE ELIOT: THE MILL ON
THE FLOSS AND SILAS MARNER
R. P. Draper

HENRY FIELDING: TOM JONES
Neil Compton

E. M. FORSTER: A PASSAGE TO
INDIA
Malcolm Bradbury

HARDY: THE TRAGIC NOVELS
R. P. Draper

HENRY JAMES: WASHINGTON
SQUARE AND THE PORTRAIT OF
A LADY
Alan Shelston

JAMES JOYCE: DUBLINERS AND A
PORTRAIT OF THE ARTIST AS A
YOUNG MAN
Morris Beja

D. H. LAWRENCE: THE RAINBOW
AND WOMEN IN LOVE
Colin Clarke

D. H. LAWRENCE: SONS AND
LOVERS
Gamini Salgado

SWIFT: GULLIVER'S TRAVELS
Richard Gravil

THACKERAY: VANITY FAIR
Arthur Pollard

TROLLOPE: THE BARSETSHIRE
NOVELS
T. Bareham

VIRGINIA WOOLF: TO THE
LIGHTHOUSE
Morris Beja

DRAMA

CONGREVE: COMEDIES
Patrick Lyons

T. S. ELIOT: PLAYS
Arnold P. Hinchliffe

JONSON: EVERY MAN IN HIS
HUMOUR AND THE ALCHEMIST
R. V. Holdsworth

JONSON: VOLPONE
J. A. Barish

MARLOWE: DR FAUSTUS
John Jump

MARLOWE: TAMBURLAINE,
EDWARD II AND THE JEW OF
MALTA
John Russell Brown

MEDIEVAL ENGLISH DRAMA
Peter Happé

O'CASEY: JUNO AND THE
PAYCOCK, THE PLOUGH AND THE
STARS AND THE SHADOW OF A
GUNMAN
R. Ayling

JOHN OSBORNE: LOOK BACK IN
ANGER
John Russell Taylor

WEBSTER: THE WHITE DEVIL AND
THE DUCHESS OF MALFI
R. V. Holdsworth

WILDE: COMEDIES
W. Tydeman

SHAKESPEARE

SHAKESPEARE: ANTONY AND
CLEOPATRA
John Russell Brown

SHAKESPEARE: CORIOLANUS
B. A. Brockman

SHAKESPEARE: HAMLET
John Jump

SHAKESPEARE: HENRY IV PARTS
I AND II
G. K. Hunter

SHAKESPEARE: HENRY V
Michael Quinn

SHAKESPEARE: JULIUS CAESAR
Peter Ure

SHAKESPEARE: KING LEAR
Frank Kermode

SHAKESPEARE: MACBETH
John Wain

SHAKESPEARE: MEASURE FOR
MEASURE
G. K. Stead

SHAKESPEARE: THE MERCHANT
OF VENICE
John Wilders

SHAKESPEARE: A MIDSUMMER
NIGHT'S DREAM
A. W. Price

SHAKESPEARE: MUCH ADO
ABOUT NOTHING AND AS YOU
LIKE IT
John Russell Brown

SHAKESPEARE: OTHELLO
John Wain

SHAKESPEARE: RICHARD II
N. Brooke

SHAKESPEARE: THE SONNETS
Peter Jones

SHAKESPEARE: THE TEMPEST
D. J. Palmer

SHAKESPEARE: TROILUS AND
CRESSIDA
Priscilla Martin

SHAKESPEARE: TWELFTH NIGHT
D. J. Palmer

SHAKESPEARE: THE WINTER'S
TALE
Kenneth Muir

MACMILLAN SHAKESPEARE VIDEO WORKSHOPS

DAVID WHITWORTH

Three unique book and video packages, each examining a particular aspect of Shakespeare's work; tragedy, comedy and the Roman plays. Designed for all students of Shakespeare, each package assumes no previous knowledge of the plays and can serve as a useful introduction to Shakespeare for 'O' and 'A' level candidates as well as for students at colleges and institutes of further, higher and adult education.

The material is based on the New Shakespeare Company Workshops at the Roundhouse, adapted and extended for television. By combining the resources of television and a small theatre company, this exploration of Shakespeare's plays offers insights into varied interpretations, presentation, styles of acting as well as useful background information.

While being no substitute for seeing the whole plays in performance, it is envisaged that these video cassettes will impart something of the original excitement of the theatrical experience, and serve as a welcome complement to textual analysis leading to an enriched and broader view of the plays.

Each package consists of:

*   the Macmillan Shakespeare editions of the plays concerned;

*   a video cassette available in VHS or Beta;

*   a leaflet of teacher's notes.

THE TORTURED MIND
looks at the four tragedies Hamlet, Othello, Macbeth and King Lear.

THE COMIC SPIRIT
examines the comedies Much Ado About Nothing, Twelfth Night, A Midsummer Night's Dream, and As You Like It.

THE ROMAN TRAGEDIES
Features Julius Caesar, Antony and Cleopatra and Coriolanus